MW01101722

CAN I BE ME

without losing you?

*"This book is written for those who long to awaken
the power of their sleeping giants within."*

Dr. P. Yam ND

CAN I BE ME

without losing you?

Chental Wilson

First Published in Canada 2013 by Influence Publishing

© Copyright Chental Wilson
All rights reserved. No part of this publication may be reproduced, stored in or introduced into a retrieval system, or transmitted, in any form, or by any means (electronic, mechanical, photocopying, recording or otherwise) without the prior written permission of the publisher. This book is sold subject to the condition that it shall not, by way of trade or otherwise, be lent, resold, hired out, or otherwise circulated without the publishers prior consent in any form of binding or cover other than that in which it is published and without a similar condition including this condition being imposed on the subsequent purchaser.

Front cover photo: Silviu Ghetie, www.ghetie.ro
Book cover design: Jessica Wilson,
www.jessicawilsonphotography.blogspot.ca
Interior typesetting: Greg Salisbury

Disclaimer: This book discusses various healing methods and spiritual techniques utilized by the author, her family, colleagues and friends. It does not recommend any medical or spiritual course of action for your specific needs. For any medical concerns, and prior to following any alternate methods of healing, please first consult your medical and spiritual practitioners of choice. Readers of this publication agree that neither Chental Wilson nor her publisher will be held responsible or liable for damages that may be alleged or resulting directly or indirectly from their use of this publication.

This book is dedicated to

My dad Cyril Luck. There were many nights I watched you in tears for the sadness of our world. I know you felt it deeply, but didn't know how to help. It was as though you were connected to something much larger than this life. Even though you were misunderstood and spent most of your life with your own thoughts, you never stopped looking for the answers to why things were the way they were. I saw the duality in you that you were determined to understand. The mystery of the human mind fascinated you, including your own, and I thank you for passing that desire to uncover the truth down to me.

To my mom, Maureen, who always loved me unconditionally and gave all of herself so freely.

To my hubby, Trevor. Thank you for having the courage and trust to go on this journey with me - not just for this book but in life. And for your undeniable love for me, you hung in there while I figured "me" out. For all my readers, Trevor never read the book until just before it went to print, he never had me change a thing and that's trust.

AND

To my two kids Phil and Jess. I couldn't wish for more consciously aware loving human beings. I want you to always know who your mother is and was so you may never wonder as I did.

Testimonials

"Chental Wilson is a genuine artist who expresses her innermost passions, dreams, fears, and desires through the essence of a personal breakthrough in her life canvas. In her recent book Chental becomes this mystical canvas, the rainbow of paints, the magical brushes and the heroic painter whom have painted the courageous and honest images of her true self, deepest aspirations and greatest passions. This book is written for those who long to awaken the power of their sleeping giants within. It is so much the truth that it is us and all that we love, experience, and create; and dare to accept the unprepared challenges to free our authentic selves from the overdue barricaded cocoons and become the ultimate spiritual warriors of life!"
Dr. Peter Yam N.D.

"It reads as though this message is coming right from the heart. I enjoyed the 'new' image idea and especially the piece about being 'a girl' That drove home the points for me. The work also left me with many questions which, for me at least, is a good thing. I want to be challenged to see things from a different perspective and again I thought you did that really well. One question that kept coming back to me was "how do we find/create/determine/agree on what balance is because it needs to be OK for the both of us-men and women--how do we maintain our uniqueness in the world and develop a much deeper, more honest and meaningful acceptance and appreciation of each other as genders without giving up too much of what makes us who we are in the first place?? I am pleased that a woman has taken on the task of helping us men understand who you are and what you need in a way that encourages us to work together to make that happen."
Jim Cloughley, Author of
"A Man's work is never done – A novel about mentoring our sons"

"*Chental brings home the essence of living from our heart's truth in a wonderfully raw, authentic voice that makes this book a remarkable page turner! Her powerful stories will inspire you to be the detective in the stories you tell yourself; to shift your perceptions and come to the greatest version of your innermost truth. Chental's pragmatic exercises are daily steps that anyone can utilize to live from a conscious place while emerging into their authentic being.*"
Karen McGregor, International Speaker,
Bestselling Author, Intuition Expert
KarenMcGregor.ca

"*In her grace Chental eloquently shares the truth of her journey from a place of courage. As she encounters the challenges of life, she views everything as an opportunity to learn, to rise, to be more. She believes the key to living rightly is to be the detective of our lives; to constantly enquire. Chental shares all that which she has come to know with a pure intent of serving. Her vulnerability is palpable.*"
Janet Love Morrison

Acknowledgements

I have always been a warrior. From as far back as I can remember, I've been a seeker of the truth. Many, many people along the way, great writers and teachers have led me to the next stage of my journey and I am truly grateful they showed up in my life when they did. This book has been a way for me to give something back.

I can't say enough about my hubby, Trevor, I love him beyond words and I truly mean that. It took me a year to put my book together and at the same time we were renovating our home. It was crazy, but he supported me through it all because he knew how important it was for me to create this book. He loves me beyond love and I have always known this: even when he didn't understand me he believed in me. He has patiently waited for me to flower and now we get to share our garden together. I was a tough cookie when we met; I think he always knew it would be a hell of a ride! Thanks honey.

I am thankful for my children, Phil and Jess and that they chose me as their mother. They have taught me so much with their truths and in the way they have been fearless in sharing themselves with me. I always said if my children grew up kind and happy within themselves, then I had done my job as a mother; they have done that and so much more. My father used to say that kids are only leant to us, we don't own them, and I never forgot his words.

To all my sisters, Annette, Yvonne, Jackie, Denise, Andree, Nicky, Sharon, and Danni, wow I don't think I could have been more loved. Truly, I am blessed to have been born into the family I was, I am truly grateful for all of you. Particularly to my sister Sharon, for without your constant support while I grew up and even when I took the limelight away from you, you still supported and loved me. I thank you all for my endless whining and questioning about life and when I was confused - you sisters were always there to listen. And I thank you for the courage you had to step into your authentic selves to show me the way.

I want to thank Ian our business partner and brother-in-law for the encouragement and understanding when we took a year off and travelled. And to his children, Amie and Jon, for I love you like my own and you too taught me so much about myself so thank you.

To my publisher, Julie Salisbury, for without her my book may never have been created and for her faith that I had something important to share. I originally wanted to write about consciousness, but she steered me in this direction for she knew intuitively that it would have been too difficult to understand; therefore, I wouldn't have been able to get my message out to the world so thank you, you were right. Thank you for always being at the end of the emails and supporting me, you are like a midwife assisting in the birth of a new child.

To my editor Lorraine Gane who worked tirelessly on my edits and who seemed to know exactly how and what I wanted to say - at times better than I did. I couldn't have produced the clarity of this book without you. Thank you for our moments in the garden on the lake; your encouragement and belief in my story and that its an important message to share; your kindness and your truth has helped me become a better writer. To Cathie and Randy Cunningham for letting us use their lovely resort on the lake for our editorial meetings.

To my second editor Janet Love Morrison, you have smoothed my pages so they flow like a great full-bodied red wine. Thank you for putting the finishing touches to my book in such a professional and timely manner and for your commitment and encouragement to and of my story.

To my office buddies Diane and Deanna, thank you for not just your dedication to our company, but for your love for me. You were always there for me in any way I needed professionally and personally, we had an office environment that was "different" but so great and I do miss that. You are my family guys.

So many people have come across my path to teach me how to step into my authentic self. It started out with my parents; my father whom I enjoyed many deep conversations about our egos, why we are here, and other dimensions. He was the first to question whether in fact this is our only reality, much to my mother's fears. My mother gave herself, she was brought up in a time where she was to support the husband and unfortunately her own dreams got pushed aside. So, mom I thank you for inspiring me to find mine again and for my love for God. You taught me about his unconditional love and for making me say my prayers every night as this has led me to a life of appreciation for all my teachers in life.

I thank Jesus for walking the earth and teaching me about unconditional love; to Anthony DeMello for teaching me how to detach; Eckhart Tolle for helping both me and my husband understand more about the ego and for his work in the world to bring awareness of it. To Eliza Mada Dalian, medical intuitive, healer, mystic, and spiritual guide, for without whom my family would not be where we are. I thank you for your compassion to help us heal our wounds of the past. As I see it, your work is of the highest importance to our world and our ability to achieve peace because you taught me that its starts with me, healing yourself from the inside out. Friends Nigel and Rose, Rick and Wendy, Betsy and Derek; and to Kindi my most conscious friend who doesn't let me get away with a thing, but in a kind and compassionate way. To Brett Wearne my yoga guru and Peter Levitt my Zen master for helping me stay grounded and centered. Master Dhyan Vimal from Malaysia for the I & I Discovery and his work he is doing around the world and for his explanation and wisdom on enlightenment.

To my naturopathic doctors first Dr.C.Alsberg, N.D.; Dr. P. Yam, N.D. and all their staff; and Linda Clark, Ph.D. To the iridologist who got me to take care of myself and the psychic / medium, Brian Robertson who helped me see more clearly, you were all such a big part of my journey. To my scientific buddies Albert Einstein who was so ahead of his time and so wise and now to Bruce H. Lipton, Ph.D. who makes complete sense to me in every way, I love your work. To Deepak Chopra for your courage and conviction to discover what you have come to know about life and to share in such an eloquent way with all of us on stage and in your books. To Dr. J. Wilson, N.D., D.C., Ph.D who without his book on adrenals, I'm not sure I would have ever figured out what was going on with my own body. You're right, adrenal fatigue is so under diagnosed. To Terra Dimock who is more amazing than words can describe, she nurtured me with her healing hands through shiatsu and for her talents and nutritional wisdom that she shared. To Sheena Bull who believed my back injuries could be healed through weight training even when others didn't and to Deb Leblanc who makes you feel like you are the most important person in her world while she is with you in her training sessions. To Helen Belot and Rasma Bertz for introducing me to the world of Sekhem and the forgiveness poem.

To all the musicians and artists who I listened to along the way who helped me to release the emotions that were otherwise locked away deep within me when words or thoughts could not release or express them. To all the authors, of all the books I have read who have paved my way for me to be me, thank you.

A special thankyou to Silviu Ghetie, thank you for your fabulous photo of the penguins and for allowing me to use it for the cover of my book. To my daughter Jessica for using her fabulous visionary talents to compile my book cover and promotional material for its release - you knew just what I wanted and it looks great, thank you! To Phil my son thank you for being you and your ability to always stay calm in a crisis and for your support while I was writing my book.

I'm sure I have missed someone very important, so if I have, please know in my heart I know who you are and know that I thank you from the bottom of my heart. I had a fear to speak my truth and through this journey with everyone's help I have transcended that fear and have discovered a greater gift: the gift of unconditional love for myself and for all of you, so thank you.

Contents

Introduction

*"When the power of love overcomes the love of power,
the world will know peace."*
Jimmy Hendrix
1942- 1970

I felt I had a responsibility to write this book. I was so fascinated by my ability to watch my thoughts and actions during my journey to awareness that I wanted to write down my "Ah ha" moments in the hopes that my experiences would resonate with others and help them to become their authentic selves.

I believed others had to change first before I could step into my authentic self. I came to discover this wasn't true. I didn't have to wait for anyone to change for me to become me, *what I believed, was stopping me from being me.* This seems so obvious, but why do most of us still compromise ourselves for the love of another, believing that's what we have to do?

Like other women, among them Elizabeth Gilbert (*Eat Pray Love*) I wanted to find out who I really was. I wanted to know what my "truth" was and what I believed, but I didn't want to leave my husband and family by going off to live in an ashram and not speak for a hundred days. I wanted to go on an inner journey within my own family.

I found myself standing at the crossroads of my life and wanting to go forward, but something was stopping me. Why couldn't I take that next step? My answer was, "Because I'm afraid that those I love won't come with me." I believed I'd be alone or they would be left behind: neither of which I could bare to allow, the choice seemed like no choice at all. But the burning desire that I could finally be one hundred percent me and keep my relationships intact pushed me forward to show me the way.

Bruce Lipton, biologist and author of *Spontaneous Evolution*, says: "Miraculous healing awaits this planet once we accept our new responsibility to collectively tend the garden, rather than fight over the turf." I support his belief. Our own individual turf, in fact, is the only one we really do have control over and how we act in the world around us; it's our personal responsibility. Once we have achieved this on the personal level, we will naturally be contributing to the global turf.

This book will show you through my stories and experiences that the most helpful tool I had during difficult times was the ability to watch my thought patterns, actions and write them down, without judgment. This is key; don't get caught up in the story. We all do this naturally all the time; however, we aren't always aware we're doing it, we most certainly don't write it down, and we likely always judge. I experienced many signposts along my path and I learned to see them clearly as I became more aware.

Eckhart Tolle describes this level of consciousness in his books: *The Power of Now* and *A New Earth*.

"Becoming aware, watching yourself act out in your own life, being a witness of your own actions and thought patterns propels you forward to become your authentic self. First you have to know what's going on within you before you can change the outcome."

It was time for me to step into my authentic self. I had realized I had left a part of me behind when I became a wife and a mother: it was time to become whole again.

My ultimate goal is for this book to reach the far corners of the Earth to lead women to become their authentic selves while still being able to have compassion towards men. We have both been conforming to other people's beliefs and beliefs passed down to us from previous generations. Not any more, it's time for the truth, our own truth.

Given I'm a woman, this book has been written from a women's perspective. To my surprise I've had a lot of interest from men who are asking the same question, can I be me without losing you? There are hidden gifts here for everyone. My objective is that we step away from the stories within our minds, from the victim mentality of "we don't have a choice" and "we are stuck with what we have." We're never stuck and we always have a choice: we have been conditioned to believe we don't. The fact is, what I believed was creating my reality.

So, if you're tired of conforming and being someone you aren't, if you say YES when you mean NO, then my story may help you find yourself while still keeping your relationships intact.

What I went through wasn't easy, there wasn't a road map for me to follow; no one gave me direct instructions. I had to let go and agree to go on this journey without knowing where it would lead. I had to have faith and trust: I had to believe. I was in search of unconditional love. Does it really exist?

Step into my shoes and come along with me on my journey to discover what I found out.

Note: Music played a big part in my evolution towards consciousness. It has a way of releasing emotions that are locked away from our mind's reach, thus every chapter is preceded by a song (at the time of publication, the rights for the lyrics were not available). If you want to know what my emotions were at any stage, listen to the song related to the chapter before you read it (listed on my website; see Author's Page). This will help set the scene in your mind and open up the emotions I was feeling.

CHAPTER ONE

Why Did I Say Yes,
When I Wanted to Say No?

Song: "Change" by Tracey Chapman

Why did I say yes when I wanted to say no? Just to get my needs met? To create safety for my kids and myself? Is that what my mother did and taught me to do? Why didn't I just speak my truth? Have I learned to manipulate and lie? Or was I simply just too afraid?

I don't believe divorce happens because we drift apart and forget to do things together after the kids come along. It seems to me, as we become moms and wives, we adjust and take on roles based on what we learned from our mothers and what has been expected of women from centuries past. All those conditioned beliefs end up determining how our own life will unfold.

The truth is, I went underground and wore a mask to protect my children and myself. Right or wrong, I did what I did because that's what I watched my mother do. She kept the peace and made sure everyone was happy: Dad, the kids, that was her job and she forgot about herself. That's what I learned to do and on some level at some point: I agreed to it. Why wouldn't I? What else did I know?

I remember spending a weekend with my sisters in 2000. One evening we went around the room asking each other the question: When are you at your happiest? My youngest sister answered first. She hesitated for a moment and then said, "When I'm painting." I could tell a part of her almost felt ashamed to admit it, even if she didn't know why, but this was her truth. My sister next to me (in age) and I gave the same answer, "When our family is happy, we're happy." I remember thinking, this is so cheesy and wrong. But I didn't say anything. It was like being aware of something you had always thought, but now after hearing it out loud you didn't agree with it anymore. My sister felt free to be happy doing something for herself and I hadn't ever thought about that possibility before. As we finished up hearing from the other sisters, I could tell my youngest sister felt as though she was being judged, and perhaps, she was. I just remember how brave she was to be so honest in spite of her eight sisters. Perhaps at the time some of us weren't even aware we weren't being as brave, or perhaps we really believed it was enough for our families to be happy. Is that what we were taught? As the youngest sister, she was always accused of being selfish and spoilt when we all lived at home. Now, when I look back, she was the only one who didn't take on our family's conditioning. If it was encouraged, she rebelled against it.

We were good girls who listened, watched, and saw how our mother was. For most of her life she sacrificed herself for the happiness of her family - and that was exactly what we were all doing. Granted, we were all happy to be that way, but we were clueless in knowing there was any other way to be. Do you know that every night my mother went off to the pub with my dad when I was little? She left my younger sister and me alone, even though it was the last thing she wanted to do. She said yes when she wanted to say no.

Why didn't she say no? She believed it would have upset our father. She believed he would have become angry and taken his anger out on her: or on us kids. So, what choice did she have? She went to the pub and left us kids to fend for ourselves. Can you imagine how hard that must have been for her? Knowing her little girls were terrified to be left alone? She had to make a choice and she believed this was the best one for us girls, so that's what she did. She did it for us. That's what I label prostituting ourselves to get what we need, be it for those we protect or ourselves. Perhaps her own mother did the same thing for the same reasons: and we did what we did because it's the only way we knew as well.

I believed I couldn't say no to my husband because I too believed he would get mad and take it out on the kids or me and then the whole house would be left in a mess. This was my job wasn't it? To keep the peace and protect the kids? I thought so. My husband isn't a violent man at all. He has never used physical force on me, our children, or anyone else for that matter. So you may ask, why was I afraid? When he raised his voice - that was enough for me. At times his energy filled the room with anger. This is what kept me from speaking my truth and it was enough to control me. This mirrored my father's behaviour and this is when I learned to be controlled by a fear of confrontation.

It goes even deeper for me. I believe in past lives. I discovered, through past life regression, that I was killed for speaking out in one of my former lifetimes. So for me, the fear was even more intense. What I believe is this: we come into this world with wounded egos that need to heal (sometimes from previous lifetimes and some accumulated from this lifetime) and it's our sole responsibility to be a detective in our own lives to find out what those wounds are in order to move forward.

I was fascinated to discover that I created my situations from my own behaviour and beliefs. Once I discovered this and grew conscious of my beliefs I could then change them, it seemed my husband would then have to make a conscious choice to accept my new way of being, as I had changed. I discovered that to become empowered was to simply embody the truth of who I am and I had to make the choice to step into all of me.

Ask yourself, how many times in your life have you said yes when you really wanted to say no? But because it would have upset your husband (or partner) and he may have taken that out on you or your kids - you just said yes to keep the peace. In the past, I would rather sacrifice myself than our children, so I would say yes when I wanted to say no.

Take sex for instance: brace yourselves ladies. You may not believe this, but I had sex twice a day with my husband for most of our married life. I can just hear the sighs, but here's the thing: Part of me believed this was my job as a wife and part of me was doing it to control the outer situations. I thought as long as I could keep my husband happy, within my own control, the whole household would be better off. To say no to sex created a negative situation and put him in a bad mood. I believed the negativity would play out into the next day and into our lives and neither the kids nor I wanted that to happen, so I said yes. Don't get me wrong, I do enjoy sex, but that was over-the-top ridiculous. I was exhausted, it was just one way I controlled him. It was crazy.

From what I've witnessed, after the kids leave home ... boom - we return to our true nature of who we really were (pre-wives, pre-kids) and we get back to our hopes our desires. How confusing is that for men? How are they to know that our yes's sometimes mean no? But because we are trying to keep the peace we compromise ourselves for peace, love, and protection. At this chapter in our lives we're wondering, what happened to our dreams? It wasn't ever about whether we still love our men; it's just now that our kids are safely on their way we can concentrate on what we wanted to be all those years ago. We don't need to be the protectors any longer.

Chapter One

I distinctly remember the day "I" returned to my body. I was sitting at our home computer doing something. Trevor, my husband, stepped into the doorway and asked me a question, (which I don't remember) and I answered him with a voice that was not, I thought, my own. I remembered having a sense of him standing there, astonished with my response and being very angry. I, on the other hand, was still wondering where that voice came from and whose it was? I pondered a moment more and then laughed to myself: It was me. I had returned from the depths of my being, from the hold of my personality to start this new path of becoming me again. My job was complete as a parent and now it was safe for me to come out. What did I want? Who am I? Exciting as it was, this was also very scary at the same time.

There was a time in history when being a wife and mother was the woman's primary role. Women didn't work outside the home; however, now we do while taking care of the husband, the kids, and the household. In the developing world, in a few countries, some women never leave the house without their husband's permission, but only because men don't want to lose control over women. They keep them in the dark, cutting them off from outside communication and making all the house rules. Women in some of these countries still believe they aren't equal to men, though, of course, it's not that they aren't, it's that they believe they aren't.

That is the problem: It's about what we, as women, believe.

The above statement is so important because as I became an observer of myself, I realized whenever I was confronted with a situation in which I wanted to say no but said yes, I usually did it, not just for safety, but a part of me truly believed this was what I was supposed to do. It was my conditioning talking, not my true self. It was very confusing.

In the Western world we think we have equality figured out, but in truth the belief many women still carry is that they aren't equal to men. I can just hear all my girlfriends saying, "That is so not true!" In our minds we have convinced ourselves that this isn't true, but our actions show it's still a belief working within us.

Just recently I bought a magazine and I was thrilled to see a whole advertising page dedicated to "Because I'm a Girl" a foundation helping girls in developing countries; however, I was also saddened to see that in 2012 girls are still fighting to be seen as an equal.

BECAUSE I AM A GIRL

Because I am a girl – I watch my brothers go to school while I stay at home.
Because I am a girl – I eat if there's food left over when everyone is done.
Because I am a girl I am the poorest of the poor.
AND YET
Because I am a girl I will share what I know.
Because I am a girl I am the heart of my community.
Because I am a girl I will pull my family out of poverty if you give me the chance.
Because I am a girl I will take what you invest in me and uplift everyone around me.
Because I am a girl I can change the world.

It just goes to show that in some parts of our world young girls and women still believe they aren't valued because of their gender. I'm thrilled we're reaching out to help empower them and change that belief.

You may say, "Well they aren't valued and it's true they aren't equal in that country." This belief is the problem women are facing around the world and this is what I wish to help them change about themselves. To believe we haven't any power over our choices or ourselves and to accept "what is" reveals a victim mentality. When you play the role of victim, you give your power away and this will not serve you. We need to understand we always have a choice, but it takes courage to step into our own inner strength and speak our truth. No one has power over you unless you give it to them. (I understand that women have been at times physically overpowered and they do not have the power to break free, I'm talking about the belief that is of the mind that we don't have the power to be ourselves). We've created stories in our minds that fuel our fears and they don't allow us to speak our truths. We need to stop believing in those stories for they are keeping us from ourselves.

We are all human beings: male and female and we are all equal. This is the very belief we need to instil in humanity. These can't just be words we read, we need to find a way to help penetrate this belief into our very beings for our lives to change. To help make this a reality, we first need to agree the stories we have been telling ourselves for centuries aren't valid any longer. We need to change the stories in our heads; we need to believe we are allowed to be ourselves; all of ourselves. This is what we were born to do and how to be in all of our relationships.

There are men who fear losing control over women. It terrifies them, for if we find ourselves we might leave them behind; change all the rules; and where will that leave them? They believe they will be powerless so they can't allow that to happen. And after all, for so long they have been the ones in control so why would they want to give that up easily?

Within both men and women there are still deep beliefs in our unconscious minds and they're running our lives. We need to find out what we really believe and not just by using our minds, but also by observing our actions: for actions speak louder than words. Observation of ourselves is consciousness and as I see it, the key.

All too often I said yes when I meant no, I believed I was protecting myself, my children or even someone else. On some level, I also believed the man was the head of the family and had the final say: he ruled the house. Even as I write this I'm surprised I believed this because I know I'm equal to my husband, but my actions certainly didn't always convey that. This conditioning could only have come from watching my parents and how they interacted; plus, an acceptance of the prevailing values of society. If you knew me at that time you wouldn't think this about me. I came across as a confident, strong, independent woman who was in complete control of her life. Yet, within me was the belief a man had the final word, so why wouldn't he believe that too? We were both conditioned to conform.

As Western women, we have learned our rights and we can fulfill our dreams. Our role isn't just to be a good wife and mother. Yet somewhere along the way, we became mothers not only to our kids, but our husbands too. When the kids leave home, you realize all you want is a partner who is capable of taking care of himself; someone to have fun with; not an adult child for you to take care of. This isn't and never was our job, but somehow we got caught up in the twist of being a mother. I'm sure it's tough for any husband to figure it all out, he may ask, "Why has it been okay for so many years?"

Men are confused. Unless you're a woman, you can't really be expected to get it and that's not the point of my book. It's what I want to enlighten the girls about.

My passion is consciousness, but what does that mean? Consciousness is the ability to observe yourself. It's what I've been doing these past eight years. It's about me being aware of my every move, my every breath, my every reaction to understand what has been going on in my evolution as a woman and this is what I want to share with all of you.

Why is it important for us to become consciousness of ourselves, especially now? We have been conditioned to believe the lies; it's time to remember the truths; it's time to empower ourselves to assist and heal our world, our children, and our men. If we women don't consciously empower ourselves (with compassion for men) to be truthful, whatever the consequences, we run the risk of keeping women in an unequal place and continuing the unbalance between the sexes. We must learn to be honest and I believe we will come to understand that being vulnerable is how we will uncover the joy hiding within us and the truth of who we are.

I used to think so many women I came across wore a mask: They weren't honest and I could tell. Did I ever think I was one of them? No. So, I found it fascinating when I discovered that I, too, had worn a mask and this was the reason I could see this in other women.

Honesty requires courage and I know it's hard to speak your truth, but remember the fear isn't real, it just feels real. At first you won't necessarily be understood and there will be confusion, but it's like being submerged in ice-cold water. At first it feels like you can't breathe, but once your body gets used to it, you will begin to feel free and empowered: that's what I want for you and for all of us.

We're able to do this for our men too because typically women have a closer connection to their inner selves. We have been trained to be compassionate, to put others before ourselves for centuries. Once we identify what we have been doing from our own untruths, we can expose ourselves to men and hopefully they too will feel safe enough to expose themselves. Then, perhaps, we can create unity between the sexes; have peace in our lives and our world. Let's face it, women already seek help through friends and therapists, but most men don't. We have to help them to understand that it's okay to expose themselves; to be vulnerable and honest; and that it's necessary if our goal is to be happy and find peace. The only way we can do this is to take off our own masks of delusion and become honest and true to ourselves. Once we show our vulnerabilities to them, they will feel safe enough to expose theirs to us. I know this to be a fact: This is exactly what happened between my husband and me.

It's so freeing to finally take off the mask.

You may feel frightened at this point, but I want you to know I was too. Yet the freedom I feel to be completely who I am today and to be able to sit here and write this book and expose every inch of my being without shame, fear, or control is euphoric. I'm not afraid. I feel happy and free and I want that for you too.

If you have ever wondered how one person can make a difference in this world, I will show you. Being empowered is contagious and affects all those around us; it's about respect on all levels of relationships. At different times in my life I heard a voice urging me to become all of whom I am, to step into myself. We all must find our inner courage.

We must all make a choice if we are to save our world and respect the feminine in all of us: men and women alike. I didn't want this to be a history book about the evolution of women and then I came across an excerpt from Eckhart Tolle's book, *A New Earth*. In his book Tolle explains why, where, and how the division and fear between the sexes emerged in the first place and he offers a better understanding of the unbalance within us, he says;

"Nobody knows the exact figure, because records weren't kept, but during a three hundred year period between three and five million women were tortured and killed by the, "Holy Inquisition," an institution founded by the Roman Catholic Church to suppress heresy. This surely ranks together with the Holocaust as one of the darkest chapters in human history. It was enough for women to show a love for an animal, walk alone in the woods and gather medicinal plants to be branded a witch, tortured, and burned at the stake. The sacred feminine was declared demonic and an entire dimension largely disappeared from human experience. Other cultures and religions, such as Judaism, Islam, and even Buddhism, also suppressed the female dimension, although in a less violent way. A woman's status was reduced to being a child bearer and man's property [see there

14

you have it, the beliefs set in history]. Males who denied the feminine, even within themselves, were now running the world, a world totally out of balance.

Who was responsible for this fear of the feminine that could only be described as acute collective paranoia? We could say, of course, men were responsible. But then why in many ancient pre-Christian civilizations such as the Sumerian, Egyptian, and Celtic were women respected and the feminine principle not feared but revered? What is it that suddenly made men feel threatened by the female?

The evolving ego in them.

The ego knew it could gain full control of our planet only through the male form, and to do so, it had to render the female powerless. In time, the ego also took over most women, although it could never become as deeply entrenched in them as in the men.

We now have a situation in which the suppression of the feminine has become internalized, even in most women. The sacred feminine, is suppressed by many women as emotional pain. In fact, it has become part of their pain-body, together with the accumulated pain suffered by women over millennia through childbirth, rape, slavery, torture, and violent death.

But things are changing rapidly now, with many people becoming more conscious, the ego is losing its hold on the human mind. Because the ego was never as deeply rooted in woman, it is losing its hold on women more quickly than on men. I believe this is why women will lead the way.

It doesn't really matter what proportion of your pain-body belongs to your nation or race and what proportion is personal. In either case, you can only go beyond it by taking responsibility for your inner state now.

Even if blame seems more than justified, [I definitely got stuck in blame] as long as you blame others, you keep feeding the pain-body with your thoughts and remain trapped in your ego. There is only one perpetrator of evil on the planet: human unconsciousness. That realization is true forgiveness. With forgiveness, your victim identity dissolves, and your true power emerges – the power of presence. Instead of blaming the darkness, you bring in the light."

My empowerment began with this awareness, for this is what I have come to know as the truth. Not only through reading it in Tolle's book, but through my own life experiences coupled with my ability to be conscious along the way. What he says is exactly what evolved within me and why I feel so passionately about the need to share it with you.

I believe it was my own personal responsibility to become conscious and then write a book to help others to do the same. And I believe, from my whole being, because of what women have suffered in the past they have the tools and the compassion to help their fellow humans grow into this new way of being through being completely honest and transparent with their thoughts.

It has been said masculine power is the power to create things that can be controlled, whereas feminine power is the power to create things beyond our control, but which our hearts most deeply long for. Within each one of us, male and female alike, it's time to balance this.

Throughout my book I refer to women as making the changes and I primarily am talking to women because I am one; however, we're all a mix of feminine and masculine energy. This means, in some cases, it will be the men in the relationship who will need to become honest and transparent to lead the way for their partners to do the same. Typically women are more feminine dominant and men are more masculine dominant, but this isn't always the case, we're all seeking a balance between the two. You might say I have contradicted myself, because in the beginning of this chapter I say, "It isn't our job to fix our husbands' problems." I would like to clarify this by adding that when we first heal our own wounded egos and step into our own power, which comes with the ability to forgive those who have trespassed against us, we are in the most natural way helping others. It's not about you doing for others; it's about you doing for yourself that empowers not only yourself, but also those you touch along the way.

I realized I couldn't love my husband as long as I resented him. So that awareness led me down a path to ask myself why I felt this resentment. I blamed him that I said yes when I wanted to say no; I blamed him that I was too afraid to speak my truth. I realized instead of constantly saying, why can't you hear me? I should have been saying, why can't I hear me? Why aren't I important enough to be heard by me? It wasn't ever about him hearing me: I just needed to start taking responsibility for my own life and what I wanted it to be. I needed to be true to myself.

This is how I believe marriage vows should be read: "We come together in this relationship to love and respect each other; to become detectives in each other's lives; to help sift through our own suitcase of wounds; to reach that place of detachment, forgiveness, compassion, and acceptance into a world of unconditional love, light, and peace."

Long after I wrote this chapter I came across a book called *Dying to be Me* by Anita Moorjani about her near death experience. Tears drifted down my cheeks when I read what she wrote, "I owed it to myself, and to everyone I met, and to life itself to always be an expression of my unique essence. Trying to be anything or anyone else didn't make me better - it just deprived me of my true self. It kept others from experiencing me for who I am, and it deprived me of interacting authentically with them."

She followed this by asking herself these questions: Why did I never stand up for myself and show the beauty of my own soul?

Why was I always suppressing my own intelligence and creativity to please others? I betrayed myself every time I said yes when I

17

meant no (God, how that one phrase turned on the taps of my tears even higher).

Why haven't I followed my own beautiful heart and spoken my own truth?

Why don't we realize this when we are in our physical bodies?

How come I never knew we are not supposed to be so tough on ourselves?

These questions were, of course, ones that I, too, had asked myself.

The Dalai Lama was quoted as saying: "The world will be saved by the Western Woman." This highlights the reality that women are emerging as the leaders of the global change movement and this is why I believe the timing of my book is important.

Remember, joy hides beneath vulnerability and happiness is our natural state of being. As you become closer to the truth, it will eventually set you free.

CHAPTER TWO

Fear to Speak my Truth

Song: "Conviction of the Heart" by Kenny Loggins

How long must we all wait to change?

We haven't been brought up to express our emotions, yet we can't deny how we feel. Why do we silence ourselves? It's time to give ourselves the chance to be heard. Too often we think what and how we feel should be kept inside like a secret only to be shared with the therapist. Perhaps it's time for a whole new way of communicating.

My thoughts had been wandering in and out about the fear to speak my truth and be honest. Last year I was involved with an online writing group and I expressed to my teacher: "I don't understand an emotion that I often have while writing, I feel I'm betraying someone. I don't mean to make anyone come across as bad. This confuses me; can you shine any light on it? I'm not responsible for their behaviour I know that, so why do I feel bad? The emotion I feel is scared, scared for me and for them, why do you suppose that is? Is it empathy because I feel they don't know what they don't know and I'm sad for them? I'm confused. If we are supposed to write freely and without reservation, then why does it scare me so? I am writing honestly because I have to in order to discover what is at the very core of me and I am, but still it scares me."

My teacher wrote back to me and I laughed. I loved his response because it reflects what we all face when it comes to honest communication.

He answered: "It's pretty simple, Chental, in many homes and psyches, we have been taught that to speak is betrayal, is dangerous, will cause us or someone else to be hurt. And so the hurting of one by another, the secrets that imprison people for their whole lives, continue. Once again, we must ask ourselves, whom does it serve to act as a prison guard, to make sure the secrets or feelings stay behind bars? What is so dangerous about saying, I like or I don't like? I did or I didn't do? You or he or she did or didn't do, or want, or believe, or thought? I say, even if you don't want to post or publish, at least write it. Where's the harm in that, in self-knowing or expression? For if THAT is not allowed, we can easily become diseased, ill, not well, whether it is guilt, or shame or physical illness. And just whom does THAT serve? It serves only the warden of the prison. And just who is that? So breathe, write, enjoy your freedom to do so and don't waste your time locked inside, there's a world here for us, we are not meant to be punished or to punish, but to enjoy."

His words felt like the song I'd been waiting to sing all my life but was too afraid. This was the permission I felt I needed to let go of my programming: my fear. Then, to write my truth was a whole other step.

I grew up in England and I was brought up in a family in which you were seen and not heard. This rule was confusing because it wasn't really true all the time. In the privacy of our own home this rule didn't seem to apply, but when we were outside we'd better adhere or else we'd be in trouble. We were polite, obedient little girls and our parents were proud of us. This was the way it was back in the 1960's and '70s. Our personalities couldn't cope with this; we saw the injustice and didn't understand why we had to adhere to those rules, it was confusing. We discovered people didn't like to be asked difficult questions; all they really want you to do is stop talking and do what they say. I have always been a detective, dissecting and digging to get to the core of a situation so I didn't adhere to that rule very well. How many times have you wanted to get to the bottom of something with someone only to find out you do all the talking, spill your beans, cry, admit your guilt, be vulnerable and humble only to be met with silence? That's a horrible feeling.

Perhaps you're ready to be a detective in your own life too. You're trying to figure out where and what went wrong, yet if the other party won't engage in a discussion, you're left with yourself once again and the old programming of guilt and doubt slips back into your psyche.

I became aware of the thoughts running through my head and how they affected my outer world. For example, with my relationships, when other parties didn't wish to resolve or discuss issues, I chose to change my belief about them. I used to feel I was being punished for crimes I didn't commit, which made me feel sad. I realized this was still making me feel like a victim, which meant I was giving my power away. So, instead of thinking about how the conversation would go or thinking I knew the other person's response, I decided to use truth to express myself regardless of the other person. In the end it doesn't matter what he or she thinks of you, it only matters that you respect yourself enough to express how you feel. I began to speak my truth even if it ended up that I might be wrong. I learned that quite often I had misunderstood and jumped to conclusions wrongly, my beliefs about a situation were out-dated. I then began to understand why I did this.

Looking back at my parents' lives, I took on their beliefs. As my parents evolved through their lives they learned and grew, but they never shared their learning with me; therefore, their beliefs became my beliefs. This pattern played out throughout my life because not only was I addressing motherhood and wifehood with those old beliefs, but also the same thing was happening with my husband. As we evolved as a couple and as parents our beliefs changed; however, because Trevor is a strong character (very convincing and very confident in the early days of our marriage) I took on most of his beliefs. Now I had my parents' and his beliefs; plus my own. I didn't realize that some of Trevor's beliefs evolved and changed, he never told me. So I carried on believing them to still be true. Later, it became quite obvious that he didn't have any idea how much I hung on to his words and beliefs. They moulded, controlled, and confused me in so many ways and at times I knew I was in conflict with myself.

I believe as we evolve, we change our ideas and ideals. We realize we don't have that much control over anyone else so we let go and back off. However, as I see it, the reason we don't share our evolution (or our change of mind) on an issue with the ones who would benefit is because there is still a part of us that believes if we do, we will give up any hope of control: just in case we still believe we can have it.

We don't tell the truth because we're worried we'll expose ourselves and give up any hope of control; thus, we remain silent. Typically, men don't do this to the extent that women do because women have been conditioned from their mothers. It's a belief passed down to us throughout history.

I believe this is the crucial point of communication breakdown between men and women - and why women confuse men. I'll give you an example. My husband and I are sailors. We bought a boat in the Caribbean and for three consecutive years we took our kids away for three months and home schooled them. Sailing is my husband's thing; I asked myself would I have a sailboat if he weren't in my life? No, so there's my answer.

This admission would have made my husband sad. I don't know why, but it's always been hard for me to tell the truth for fear of upsetting him. He wants me to love sailing as much as he does, but I don't. I love being on the water at quiet anchorages; I love exploring new places; I love the boating life; and spending such quality time together as a family; however, the actual act of sailing I don't love. It's a lot of work. I don't like heeling over and worrying if we'd all be dumped into the water.

I hated sailing between islands during the dark nights and having to be on watch; it's just not fun for me. There was a time in our marriage when he talked about sailing around the world for a year or two. This freaked me out. I thought I can't do it, I just won't be able to cope, I'll hate it. I tried to tell him, but he was convincing me that it would be fun and I'd like it. This is where he always got me. I trusted his ideas and beliefs more than my own. I let him change my mind because I didn't want to upset him. I let him convince me on some things, but this was just too big. I knew I wouldn't be able to do it, so how was I going to get out of it? He and his brother would talk about it; they read numerous books on people who had done it and went to boat shows. I really believed he was going to do it and I was just expected to come along.

I know it seems silly, but I would talk to my sister about how I was going to get out of doing this. I seriously wondered if the only way to get out of it was through divorce: extreme thinking or what? Of course I didn't want a divorce, but I believed he would make me go. How does that work? It's crazy. I spent years wondering how and when this might actually come about. Well, he began to realize I wouldn't ever sail across an ocean and he accepted that about me. But instead of telling me, for years I believed he still wanted me to go and I continued to create situations to deflect the idea. Why didn't I just say no? Why didn't I believe that my no would be enough? Why was I so afraid of upsetting him? He had accepted and let go of the fact I was wasn't going to sail around the world, but I was still stuck in the old belief.

This pattern was happening in many of my beliefs, they were old and had changed but nobody informed me of that. It's so interesting that our beliefs stay frozen from the time we first encountered them. The discovery of my beliefs fascinated me because questions remained at the core of it all: Why did I constantly let people change my mind? Why did I follow theirs more than my own? I had a fear of upsetting others. It was easier to go against myself and let others win. I conformed more than not, I was too afraid of speaking my own truth. The book, *Smile at Fear: Awakening the True Heart of Bravery* by Chogyam Trungpa has a great paragraph that spoke so strongly and helped me to climb out of doing my pattern.

"Once there was a young warrior. Her teacher told her that she had to do battle with fear. She didn't want to do that. It seemed too aggressive; it seemed unfriendly. But the teacher said she had to do it and gave her the instructions for the battle. The day arrived. The student warrior stood on one side and fear stood on the other. The warrior was feeling very small, and fear was looking big and wrathful. They both had their weapons. The young warrior roused herself and went toward fear, prostrated three times, and asked, 'May I have permission to go into battle with you?' Fear said, 'Thank you for showing me so much respect that you ask permission.' Then the young warrior said, 'How can I defeat you?' Fear replied, 'My weapons are that I talk fast, and I get very close to your face. Then you get completely unnerved, and you do whatever I say. If you don't do what I tell you, I have no power. You can listen to me, and you can have respect for me. You can even be convinced by me. But if you don't do what I say, I have no power.' In that way, the student warrior learned how to defeat fear."

This described me for so many years. People who were bigger, louder, seemingly smarter, and who had bigger energy overpowered me to the point at which I just didn't feel I could speak my own truths. It always felt easier to conform and worry about me later. It really wasn't until Trevor and I went on our motorcycle trip to Europe that my true self had had enough of conforming and wanted to change things. It was time for the real me to step forward and participate fully in life. I had been hiding from myself; hiding from my own truths.

So with this new understanding: that what I believe to be true might not necessarily be so, I didn't enter into a conversation thinking that I knew the answer. Now, I go into a conversation believing it will be a pleasant one, not one of conflict, and it's amazing the difference this makes. If I have positive thoughts going into the conversation, then it seems this is what I get back and vice versa. It gets back to the fact that what we believe creates our reality: so my advice, start believing how you actually want your reality to be. If you are afraid going into a conversation, it's very likely it won't turn out very well for you. Remember, your energy hits the airwaves long before your spoken word does, so stay calm and go in believing it will all work out fine.

Peace was my addiction. I realized I had to stop conforming as it only left me feeling like a victim, which only stole my power away from me. Previously, I would conform to achieve peace, but this was getting me into trouble and making me feel I had become something I wasn't. I was in conflict with myself. I had to become honest even if I wasn't going to be right. Going into a conversation I couldn't possibly know the outcome, but at least by being honest it would be revealed to me whether I needed to learn and reflect about myself. I loved the exposure and vulnerability of finally starting to understand what was going on.

In Jill Bolte Taylor's book called, *My Stroke of Insight,* she talked about breathing: When something or someone triggers your ego and you feel the need to defend, it works to breathe for at least ninety seconds because by that time you will have realized that there really is no danger and therefore no need to be afraid.

I agree. When you are verbally attacked your body responds as if you're being attacked, with adrenaline, and this makes you have a heightened sense of awareness. If you breathe for a while, the breath is letting your body know that all is okay. Once the ninety seconds is over, then your body relaxes and you can respond without fear. I have witnessed and experienced this many times with others and myself. Bringing awareness and verbalizing it out loud in the moment is so helpful. Up until now most of us haven't communicated in this manner, but once you start this practice, others will follow. You become aware that the fear isn't real and to talk dissipates it. The more you use the technique, the easier it gets. It's a great tool to teach your children, breathe, relax, and then respond.

When you know you're right for you, you don't have to convince others, just be a witness. Any time you recognize you are defending yourself, realize your ego has been challenged, not you. You are not your ego. Your ego is the part of the self that (when in fear) acts like a child protecting itself, quite irrational at times, usually aggressive and attacking. Your ego has been activated because you feel afraid. The questions to ask yourself are: Why am I feeling afraid? What am I afraid of? In other words, go inward, not outward for the answers. How we react to the outside world is a reflection of what is going on inside us.

James Allen wrote in his book, *As a Man Thinketh*, "He who has conquered doubt and fear has conquered failure. His every thought is allied with power and all difficulties are bravely met and wisely overcome. Thought allied fearlessly to purpose becomes creative force."

Time and time again we've been told by many wise people before us that fear isn't real, it's just a human emotion, go into it, and don't run away from it. Fear has a gift for you, even if it doesn't feel that way at the time. It takes courage to go into the fear, but every time you step into it, it gets easier because you prove to yourself through your own experiences it is not real.

A warrior knows that everyone is afraid of everyone else. This fear reveals itself in two ways, through aggression or through submission. They are two sides of the same problem. When faced with someone who fills him with fear, a warrior is conscious that the other person shares the same uncertainty. However, instead of retreating the warrior uses fear as an engine.

My advice: Become a detective and find out what you're afraid of. Go into the fear with honesty as your guide. Don't run from fear. Are you aware that once you release fear into the air, it's there for another to intercept it and take on? The person receiving will think there is something to be afraid of without knowing what it is. Therefore, be very careful and mindful when you release your fear. And if you do release fear, warn the other person you are feeling afraid even if you don't know why. Then, at least he or she can be prepared and not be so afraid. We have an energy field that surrounds us, it holds our beliefs and emotions; therefore, if we emit love or fear when we come into contact with others their energy field picks it up. That is why sometimes we don't even need to speak: yet we already have sensed what is going on with other people.

When I'm in front of another with whom I start to feel afraid I say out loud to them: I don't know why, but I suddenly feel afraid. Then I take a couple of deep breaths and continue the conversation. This does two things: One, it gives you a moment to take those deep breaths (that ninety second reprieve to let your body know you're actually okay and not in danger) and two, it lets the other person's ego stand down to do the same thing. This helps once you start to actually talk because the body's fight or flight response has been acknowledged, but it's also been told to stand down which is really important. People will be uncomfortable the first few times you try this, but as you practice it others may follow too.

A couple of years ago I had an experience I couldn't explain. As I headed for work one morning, full of the joys of spring, I opened the office door and was hit with a heavy negative energy. Two people sat before me and I sensed they were discussing something very serious and whatever it was, the police were involved. I couldn't make sense of it in the moment, so as I entered the office, I stopped, looked at them both and realized I had just witnessed a kind of premonition and quickly darted to my office. Immediately after, one of them came to see me when she realized how distressed I was. She kept telling me it was going to be okay, yet I didn't feel it would be. I was still trying to understand what had just taken place. My body had received information, yet my brain didn't have a chance to catch up or understand how this could have happened. Regardless, I clearly knew what they were discussing and it didn't feel good.

I needed to leave the office for some air so I decided to go to my parents' graves and sit to see if they could help me understand. My mother was always frightened by these kinds of experiences, but my father understood them as he had experienced them himself. It came to me that the premonition I had just experienced was, in fact, what used to happen to my father all the time. Unfortunately, my dad never fully understood what was actually happening. He used to explain that when he was faced with this kind of situation, it was the devil that had taken possession of another's body and it was his job to exorcize it out of that person. That's a scary thought. Well, I can tell you the "exorcism" was never pretty and it scared the hell out of everyone, especially the poor soul who it had taken hold of, leaving him confused and more damaged than helped. Anyway, as I sat there in the graveyard, I realized I had picked up this information in the energy field when I entered the room. I knew this is what my father experienced but I also knew that I wasn't going to follow in his footsteps with the exorcist thing, but instead help the person to understand what I had just experienced. In other words, my job in all of this was to be the detective. I had witnessed ego and fear in another and it was my job to help her to understand that she was acting out of her fear. It wasn't her true self. My work was to simply bring awareness to what I felt in the room.

This poor girl knew she had upset me, yet she hadn't said a word to me. I went back to work later that afternoon and decided to tell her we both needed some time to decide what had happened and we would discuss it later. She apologized for upsetting me and given that I still was unsure of what exactly happened, I said okay and left it at that.

The next day I went into work and I knew by this time that I needed to learn how to handle these situations with love and compassion. I told her what I had felt and how it shocked me as much as it did her. We laughed with relief; we were still okay and friends. I shared the story of my father and of how he handled these situations, and then I shared how I wanted to handle it. We chatted about how clever the ego is, how convincing it can be and the need to keep it in check. You can act from either love or fear, not both. You have to ask yourself whenever you're making a decision: Is this coming from love and compassion? Or is this coming from fear and the need to be right or have revenge? We all know which one is the right choice; it's just that we don't give ourselves the time or permission to choose: instead we react out of fear. As it turned out, this is exactly what she was doing. They were discussing a family issue and she was deciding how to handle it, but she was in fear and angry. She knew the decision she was making in that moment would affect a lot of people and could be irreversible. I felt nothing good would come of her decision. My awareness of this, as I entered the space, was to share my intuition so she could take some time and choose how she would handle this from a place of love instead of a place of fear.

If the true self can't be hurt, only the ego can. In hindsight, I could have taken some deep breaths and realized that this was my ego trying to protect me. My ego was angry that I had to deal with the situation as I walked in the office door - especially when I was in such a good mood at the time, but I didn't need protecting. I was just fine.

I decided the next time it happened I'd just breathe and verbally share what was going on within me right there and then. This is what awareness brings to a situation; the light where there is darkness and confusion. Later that day, I told her that I believed we are the truth seekers, just like small children before they have been conditioned. Plus, I'm convinced together we have walked this Earth before. I had learned a great deal from this experience and it answered a lot of my childhood questions about my own father.

Shortly after I watched, a documentary called, *I Am* by Tom Shadyac, who also produced, *Liar Liar*, starring Jim Carrie. He had a bicycle accident that left him with a concussion beyond repair and it sent him into depression. One day his depression miraculously lifted, so he decided to do something much more useful with his life. He went around the world asking different spiritual leaders: What's wrong with our world?

On the trip he shows a clip in which he went to the American based Heart Institute that researches energy fields and thoughts and how they relate. It confirmed what I'd experienced in the office that day. Researchers sat a man in a chair and on the table in front of him was a meter that measured frequencies with its two wires plugged into a container full of yogurt. The meter wasn't connected in any way to his body. The man was told to think about something he was angry about, so as he thought about his divorce and the lawyers: the meter went sharply down. When he thought about something nice, it went the other direction. When the man relaxed the meter stayed in the middle. Indeed, we all effect one another's space and knowing this would help us understand feelings we sometimes have, but can't explain. In other words, when scientists tell us we are all connected to one another, this is what they mean. So if you have ever walked into a space, and felt as though someone in the room had an issue, you're likely correct, because what we think gets projected into our field of energy around us and then others who enter that space can pick it up. Children are very good at this.

I now understood why and what I had been feeling for many years with my husband and sisters. As soon as I was in their presence, I was picking up their fears: it would just hit me. Their thought would be released into their energetic field and then when I came into the same space, my energetic field picked it up and I could feel it too. This was exhausting. Many of you will relate to what I'm saying because all humans can do this even if they are not aware of it. However, if this realization of what has just happened and isn't talked about, a misunderstanding or fear can build up which makes for very poor communication, resentment, or anger. We don't know what people are thinking. We may pick up their emotions. As a result, I decided when I'm with another person and I'm feeling something I can't make sense of, I choose to be open and honest and say so to communicate clearly. Some people are shocked that I can sense their thoughts and some are glad I can do this as it allows what they're feeling to be dispersed, so it's a win-win for both of us. This is something we aren't comfortable doing, but this is exactly what I believe we need to start doing more often. Trust your intuition.

The same thing happened with my sister who I was in business with - which was one of the reasons I decided to leave our company where I'd worked for twenty-eight years. I just couldn't live in that field of energy anymore; it bothered my own sense of balance. My sister, who is two years older, had worked with me for most of our lives but there was always something about her I couldn't understand. There was a feeling of fear I sensed from her, of what I didn't know. Later on, during a writing class I was asked to write about the perception of a mother's love which turned out to be interesting because I discovered where this fear came from within her.

Notes left behind

It's been six years since my mom passed away and every so often she comes back into my life to help me to grow and move on. By that I mean I'll be doing something and then all of a sudden she will be on my mind for a few days and then after a while I will have realized she has come to help me on the next stage of my journey.

When I was researching names for this book, I remembered that when my mom passed away, I was going through her things and she, too, had started to write a book about her life. She was going to call it "Ten to One." She thought it would reach a broader audience as people would think it was about gambling. So I emailed the title to some friends the other night to see if they got what that means and then I remembered where I put the beginning pages of her book and reread it.

She had only gotten three pages written, but in those pages you could already feel this was a woman who had been through hardship and pain, but who managed to be graciously thankful and grateful for her life. She talked about the birth of her first child, her husband going off to war and surviving, and then the love she had for all the other eight children and finally her most precious gift of all, her husband.

She writes, "I had survived all the bombings of the home countries, and my husband had been through the ordeal of serving six years in the merchant navy, being involved in Atlantic Convoy and the D-day Invasion, so I suppose the peacefulness of this moment seemed too good to be true.

Understandably, my mother spent a great part of her life living in fear. Can you imagine having nine girls in those times? Can you imagine your husband going off to war and never knowing if he would ever come back? I can't. I am just beginning to understand the magnitude of her fear, how alone she must have felt, what she has taught me, and the courage she has given me.

A mother's love for her child can come out in mysterious ways. My mother gave me unconditional love. We moved back to England (from Canada) when I was eleven and those years were tough on her. She didn't want to make the move, she had to work in a factory, and she was very unhappy. I remember coming home from school and she would be in the living room sleeping all the time. She was depressed; she missed her life in Canada. We were living in the country and for me that was great, but for her she felt isolated and alone. My mom was too depressed to watch over me so I was free. I had the freedom to be me and to grow with a lot of space around me. That was her gift to me. On the other hand, some of my sisters would beg to differ. She needed some of them, she relied on them, and because they could sense the sadness and fear in her during those times they were at her beck and call. The sisters who were by her side were empathic to her and felt sorry for her, so they helped in any way they could and for that they had to endure her emotional pain. It's hard to explain, she loved them with her whole heart; however, it didn't always appear that way. They were the ones she would speak harshly to and they would be confused by her actions as they were good little girls and did what their mother asked. I, on the other hand, was off in my own world. I was too young to know anything different.

It wouldn't be until our mom died that my older sister would tell me my mother worried about me and asked her to watch over me. Can you imagine being asked to watch over another family member when you yourself are only two years older and feel you need watching over too? This sister did what her mother asked and watched over me. I was oblivious to all of this; I was just being me. Until this day I don't know why my mother was so afraid for me, but the only explanation I have come to is that I take after my father in some ways and she saw how people treated him because he was different. He spoke his truth no matter what, he couldn't be swayed from that and she also knew there was a deep sadness in him. He had compassion for this world and I think some part of her saw that in me, too, so she worried about me.

This would mean that for many years, somewhat as if a contract had been drawn between us, my sister and I would stick very close to each other in life and business. I never understood why I could always feel fear in her. I never knew what she was afraid of all the time. I would just bounce along in life with my bull-in-a-china-shop way and be just fine, but I could always feel her fear, never knowing where it was coming from. I have finally come to understand her fear for me was passed onto her from our mother.

I never allowed anyone to read my writing while I was working on my book because I didn't want to be influenced, but this piece I felt I had to give to her, not really understanding why. At work one day I slipped it to her and I couldn't have been more surprised by her reaction. She was speechless and so touched to the point she couldn't speak. Once she collected herself, she came back into my office and said, "Thank you, I have to tell you that my heart leapt out of my chest when I read that."

So you see, I never knew what she knew. She couldn't explain it to me for whatever reasons were her own, yet by me bringing my own awareness to why I couldn't work at the office anymore I released the burden our mother had put on her to watch over me all those years ago. Even if she wasn't fully aware of it before, it had a hold on her. We had finally broken the unspoken contract between us and we both felt so much happier. She doesn't have to be afraid for me anymore and now I know where her fear was coming from. There are just so many hidden gifts in awareness.

Becoming a detective in my own life has unlocked so many of my own childhood secrets and as I share them with the rest of my family; their secrets are unlocked for them. It's an amazing gift to give one another. This is why I feel we have been hiding from ourselves for far too long and it's time to be vulnerable and seek the truth: as it will surely set us free.

CHAPTER THREE

Sins of Our Fathers

⟡

Song: "Fiddle N Bow" by Bruce Guthro

I loved my father dearly. I loved his big hands and the energy that vibrated out of them into my face when he cupped them around my cheeks. It felt like nothing could ever go wrong and he would make sure of it. He used to call me "Titch" and tell me not to worry so much. At that time we lived in a large mansion in a village called Louth in Lincolnshire, England. It was grand, beautiful, mysterious, and haunted too. I have a lot of fond memories from living there; the gardens and the secret passages; and my Dad playing his violin (until one day at work when he caught his fingers in a machine and lost the use of some of them for some time). When they healed he picked it up again (he played quite well) and began to teach my sister and I to play classical music when I was eleven years old. I'm pretty sure I perfected only one piece to his liking, the one I played solo at my high school for some musical event. He taught us how to care for our violins by oiling them with walnuts, how to get the oil out and then rubbing them into the grain. He treated those violins like they were works of art. I remember putting them into their blue-velvet sleeves before placing them into their cases. I knew they were very precious to him, plus they were very old instruments. When I hear the sound of a violin, even to this day, I am immediately connected with my dad. I feel as though his heart is open to mine and we are in harmony with each other.

We were renting that house so when Dad finished building our own house in the country, a year later, we moved into the new one. Life there wasn't much fun for my mom. My dad was happy, given he always loved to build things and garden, but our mom was lonely. We lived way out in the country with only two other houses across the road from us and then it was at least five miles to the closest village. We were surrounded only by farmland and Mom was used to living in a large town in Canada, she missed her home and life there. As a teenager, when I came home drunk from parties, dad would be the one to put me to bed. My mother would be furious, rambling on at me the whole way up the staircase. When I had toothache, he would be the one who rubbed whisky on my gums. We would watch Sci-Fi shows together, work in the garden, build greenhouses, and create other projects. These are my fondest memories of my father.

Years after I was married, when I would visit him, his face would always light up. It's the one thing every kid wishes to happen with their parents, it felt nice and I felt lucky to have this kind of relationship with him. He never tired of me dropping by for a visit and we would talk for hours. Some days our conversation was as simple as discussing the flowers he planted in the garden and other times it was deep and complicated as we ruminated on Einstein, quantum physics, different realities, religion, and philosophy. It didn't matter; I loved it. He was always consciously aware when he spoke to me. I don't remember a harsh word he ever said to me in my life. However, I remember the harsh words he spoke to my mother and my sisters. It wasn't kind and I never knew why he did this. I didn't have the courage to ask him. My dad liked to be right. Even though he talked about the ego all the time with me, he never quite got that he himself had a strong one. I think some of my sisters challenged him and perhaps that's why he got mad at them.

We spent the next eight years living in England until my parents eventually made the move back to Canada in 1982 and built a home on Salt Spring Island, BC. In 1981, Trevor and I got married and also moved back to Canada. I would often pick my parents up take them for lunch in Duncan, which was a 30min ferry ride and we would spend our time together going to garden shops and bookstores. My father developed colon cancer in 2000 and after that it became too difficult for him, now that they're both gone I cherish those memories.

Dad never liked doctors so, of course, he avoided going to find out what was wrong with him until it was too late. He was stubborn and didn't like to take conventional medicine unless it was absolutely necessary, so he made his own home remedies such as castor oil rubs for his stomach problems. I remember the day we took him to the hospital. He was such a trooper and never made a fuss with the nurses about what they had to do because I think he knew how bad a shape he was really in. As he walked down the corridor of the hospital, he left a trail of blood behind him. I felt so sad for him; he would have been embarrassed had he'd known. He was such a proud man. The cancer had gone on for too long and the tumour had gotten too big. Right then and there he had to have an operation to remove some of the colon and be fitted with a colonoscopy bag. Even then he was okay with it all; he took it in his stride. He was in hospital for a week and then we took him home. For the next year, we took turns taking him to the hospital on the mainland for radiation therapy. Later that year, when I was due to leave on one of our Caribbean boating trips, my father became so sick that the doctors said he wouldn't last more than a few months. I decided to cancel to be with him. After all, he was my father. How could I leave him? All the other girls would be there. I had to tell Trevor I wanted to postpone our trip. He wasn't thrilled, but this was my dad who had been there for me my whole life. I wanted to be there for him right to the end. I couldn't bear the thought of coming home with him gone.

After I had made my decision I thought about bringing my parents to our home to take care of them as watching my dad suffer was so hard on my mom. Then, one day I woke up and knew I had to go on my trip: it was the strangest feeling. My mind was telling me to stay, but something else was saying 'You don't need to be here, you should go on your trip'. It took a few days for me to come to terms with this, but it just felt right. I didn't know why this had come about, but I trusted my feeling. This is what I had to do. I think I confused my sisters. I'm not sure what they were all thinking, no one said anything to me, but even I thought it was odd. So Trevor and I made arrangements to travel the Caribbean with our two kids. The whole time I was making the arrangements it felt surreal, it was as though someone else was doing the actions and I was watching them - like I was being guided.

The hardest part was saying goodbye to my dad knowing he wouldn't be there when I returned. I bought a card and a little picture, which I still have today, it reads: "When the mind is quiet, the heart speaks." As I walked into the house that day to say my final goodbye, I could smell the odour of death. It's an awful rancid smell like nothing else I had ever encountered. I went into the living room where he was lying down. His bed was beside the window so he could look out at the garden. He was awake and as usual always put on a good front. He smiled at me and said, "Hello dear." I pulled up a chair and gave him my card.

I had written a poem for him, thanking him for being in my life and loving me the way he did. I told him I had learned about taking care of my body from him, not because he was a good teacher, but because he was a lousy one. He smiled, knowing what I meant. I told him he never took care of his physical side; he was far more interested in his spiritual side leaving the poor human body to carry him around without regard for what it needed. In truth I was a little mad at him for not taking better care of himself. His body had become tired and ill. He had spent his last days as an assistant to the priest at our local church; even seeing people who needed help until shortly before he died. For him, it was just more important to help others. My dad was a big fan of Edgar Cayce, the American psychic who died before his time who also helped others before himself. We tried to get Dad to save his strength for himself and our family, but he insisted on seeing people right to the end if they needed him. My last words to him were: "How will we communicate when you are gone?" The answer immediately came to me, I know, I will write and you will come through in my writing, that's what we will do. Many times during the writing of this book, I have felt my father doing just that.

I remember one Sunday, before Dad became too ill to assist the priest, when some of my sisters and I went to church as we knew he would be helping at the mass. I think for the first time and one of us asked him if he was nervous. He seemed annoyed to be asked that question. I had a sense he wasn't nervous; in fact, the work felt very natural for him. I understand what he was thinking that day. I, too, have realized I didn't step into all of me until I could let go of my own family's fears for me. They weren't my fears, but they confused me and made me feel as though I should be afraid of something. It's like our family had this belief we should hide from life, to stay safe, and perhaps in our own way some of us were still doing that including me at that time. Finally, at seventy-seven years of age, he came into his own without any fear and did what he had always wanted to do.

He knew Mom was terrified of losing him to the church. I suppose my sisters and I were, too, not for him but for our mom.

We headed off on our trip to the Caribbean and it was about two months before I made my final call to speak with him. I checked my emails as much as I could to see how he was doing.

In 2001, email access in the eastern Caribbean was sparse at best. Every time I came across a church, I would go in and pray for my dad, my mom, and my sisters.

Then, one day, after we pulled into Rodney Bay and went to town I found a pay phone and called home. It was about six o'clock in the evening. My mom said she was okay, but she was so glad I had called. She said my father hadn't eaten for ten days; he had drunk only a few sips of water. She believed he was waiting for me to call. She thought he didn't want to go without saying goodbye one last time. She told me he was in a coma and on morphine, but I still wanted to talk to him anyway. I wanted him to hear my voice. She put the phone to his ear and I shouted to him, "I love you dad, have a safe journey, we will be together again one day." I was shouting so loud my husband had to tell me to be quieter. I knew dad's condition, but I wanted to make sure he knew it was me who had called and I told him I loved him again. Boy, that was a hard phone call. I knew those were the last words I'd ever say to my dad.

I will never forget that day. We went back to the boat and the kids sat up on the boom watching the stars that night. I told them they may see a shooting star and if they did, it would be grandpa going home. The next morning I went to check my emails. During the night one of my sisters had written, "Dad has been called home." I was so confused. Did that mean he was at the hospital and had gone home? No, he had died. She continued, "After you phoned, a few hours later he woke from his coma, he told Mom he loved her and passed away." Mom said, "He was waiting for your call." It meant a lot to me that I was able to speak to my father, even if he was in a coma. I know he heard me.

Something I didn't mention: My father never told my Mom he loved her. Every time she asked why he never verbalized it, he told her she should know by his actions that he loved her. He said it was her ego that needed to hear this, not her true self. I know he really believed this was better for her, but all she ever wanted was for him to say, "I love you". I think because of what we believe, we try to influence others with our ideas. I know I used to feel this way about my own husband because he's a lot like my mom and needed positive affirmation of my love. I felt like my dad, but knowing how much his last dying words meant to my mom made me realize it's not fair to Trevor. Before, my own ego was telling me the same as Dad's; spouses should just know. What are we achieving if we are causing others pain and for the simplicity of saying: I love you? Why did I build such a wall up around that one? Well, I figured out it was my own ego.

Before we left on our trip I bought my dad a card and wrote what I wanted my friend Paula to read out at his funeral. I left instructions with my mom to play Bruce Guthro's song, *Fiddle and Bow* during his funeral, but to my disappointment and surprise my mother didn't carry out my wishes. Her Catholic conditioning told her this song wasn't appropriate to be played in a church. Her decision hurt me to my core. I couldn't physically be there and this was my way of saying thank you and goodbye to my dad, but because it wasn't proper, she wouldn't do it. It felt as though she chose the church over me.

Another thing I discovered, which ties into all this, is that my mother feared my father leaving her for the church. It gets even clearer, years later one of my sisters told me the real reason my mother was afraid was because my dad and I would talk into the wee hours of the night. Was she afraid for Trevor? That I might leave Trevor for the church or some other spiritual cult? I'm not my dad and I don't believe we need to join a religion and leave our families to be teachers of consciousness. As I see it, we just need to be in touch with our authentic selves and that is my journey: to learn and teach. I've never had a fear of needing to leave my relationship to be able to do this. It's interesting how my mother's fears played out into my life, not to protect me, but my husband. It's strange because I'm sure she believed she was protecting me, but I believe she was protecting herself, unknowingly of course, she didn't want me to be alone. Every time I believed I was doing something to protect another, it was really to protect myself from the anxiety I would have when others would be hurt or upset, I just couldn't bear it.

It's funny, but on reflection I remember wanting to go on a retreat and Trevor didn't want me to go. Whenever Trevor wanted to go off biking with the guys or go on another type of adventure, I would always say go for it, have fun - but the same wasn't granted back to me. One time I wanted to go to Hollyhock on Cortes Island for a long-weekend retreat. I mentioned it to him and he didn't like the idea. Finally, I asked him what was the problem, what was he afraid of? (This was years before anything became clear to either of us.) He thought a moment and very clearly told me: "I'm afraid that when you come back, there won't be a place for me." I replied: "That's silly of course there will, I will always love you." "No," he said: "It's not that you won't love me, it's that there won't be a place for me in your new world."

Although this surprised me, I was happy he was able to articulate it. Needless to say, I didn't end up going on that retreat, which was typical of me at that time. Now it seemed this was Trevor's fear, too, that I might leave him for the church or some other spiritual cult.

Even though my Dad loved and was kind to me, I learned growing up in our large family he wasn't like this with everyone. He drank too much and got angry for no reason at all, it seemed he became unconscious of his actions. And because there was a house full of girls, our mom was always trying to protect us from his anger. I learned to conform to keep Dad happy and quiet: to keep the peace.

My dad was unconsciously aware of how he treated others, but not everyone. So you see, loving someone isn't enough. He loved me, yet I still had to witness how he treated others and that played a role in my beliefs and my life: it became my wound. As a result, those beliefs kept me from being true to myself later in life.

Parents who argue have such a huge effect on children. Even if the parents think they are hiding their true feelings, the children still feel them. Eckhart Tolle says, "Children are not fooled by parents who try to hide their own pain-body from them, who say to each other, 'we mustn't fight in front of the children.' This usually means while the parents make polite conversation, the home is pervaded with negative energy. Suppressed pain-bodies are extremely toxic, even more than openly active ones and that psychic toxicity is absorbed by the children and contributes to the development of their own pain-bodies."

How sad no one told us about this so we could prevent our own children from having to take on our pain bodies.

My father encountered many challenges in his life. He grew up in a very strict Catholic family; by all accounts he was abused as a child. He was labeled stupid because he was dyslexic; thus, he was very conscious when he wrote. Right up until the day he died, my mom always did the writing in our household. My sisters told me he was put in a cupboard for punishment and sent off to the navy at a very young age. He carried so much pain, which everyone in the family could feel. I thought I was the only one to sneak under the radar, so to speak, with regards to my connection with my father. We had had a great relationship and I knew he always loved and never doubted me. I was lucky that way. It was a surprise when I realized that I, too, fell victim to the "sins of my father".

He was a man with a lot of energy and I don't mean physical energy. It was an energy we kids could feel easily. We knew he had a big heart and was kind and gentle underneath, but unfortunately he expressed himself from anger too often. When you looked deep into his eyes, you could feel a man with a lot of pain and fear; most likely, from the "sins of his father".

He had spent time in the British Navy during World War Two. He lied about his age and fortunately he wasn't sent to the front lines because he knew he could never kill anyone. He got married, brought up nine girls, went through a bankruptcy, and finally decided to get out of England in the 1960's and move his family to Canada.

It was the summer in1973 our dad moved half of the family back to England. Those were rough days. He got a job he didn't like and so did my mother. She hated England: coming from Vancouver it was cold, damp, and depressing, and she never did settle there. Then, in 1982, they came back to Vancouver and eventually moved to Salt Spring Island which they both loved.

My father carried a lot of pain along his journey and us girls could feel it growing up. Although his behaviour wasn't always okay, on some level we forgave him. What choice did we have? We were kids and didn't have the tools to deal with it; we were in survival and protection mode.

This brings me to my point. You get to choose how you're going to be in a relationship with someone. If you've grown up knowing a Jekyll and Hyde type personality, then it shouldn't be a surprise that you may come across the same in your own relationships; kind and gentle one minute and off-the-wall and confusing the next.

It was when my dad drank that the preaching from the mantle about hell and damnation began. How confusing is that to a child? I'm sure my mother was always trying to keep the status quo. I'm sure you can imagine, in such a big family, the emotions must have been flying. He would rant on about aliens and past lives and religious preaching and whoever was home that night had to sit and listen until my mother would come in and send us off to bed. That was usually a relief for most of us. I, on the other hand, was always quite fascinated with his stories. I showed an interest, so I never felt he was preaching to me. I think it's because I wasn't afraid, plus it meant I got to stay up later. The movie, *Mary Reilly*, with Julia Roberts was a great rendition of the story of Jekyll and Hyde. I liked how the movie showed how a personality can conflict; thus, only through consciousness and awareness of this knowing can balance be restored within the person. If we're acting differently from our true self; first we need to have an awareness. Most of us are not aware of this fact, my father certainly wasn't.

Many years after my father died, I had a dream about him in which he was asking for my forgiveness. I told him he had been a great father to me and I didn't need to forgive him, but perhaps he needed to forgive himself. The next day, I had another dream in which I was in fear. Someone had broken into our home and was trying to kill us. I had to prostitute myself to trick these people so we could all escape. When I woke up, I thought this was symbolic. Was this what my sisters and I had been doing all our lives? Had we just been keeping everything under the radar like our mom did for the sake of the children?

I'm quite sure what made all us girls empathic and able to feel the pain of others was due to living with a reactive father. Perhaps we had few boundaries or maybe none. Perhaps we chose partners with their own pain; likely from "the sins of their fathers". Everyone has a form of dysfunction going on in family life, so I don't suppose it would have mattered whom we picked. There would have been some form of living under the radar for the sake of the children; however, had I the awareness of how my own mother handled this dysfunction at the time. I could have made different choices in my own life about how to deal with conflict and unconscious behaviours. Isn't it sad that "for the sins of our fathers" we didn't realize this was even happening?

Finally, when I woke up after my dream, I laid there thinking about my dad and remembering he had asked me to forgive him. I realized he wasn't asking me to forgive him for anything that actually happened between us, he was asking for forgiveness from the "sins of his father" which in turn became his sins. He never knew he was living an unconscious life; that is until after he died. This may seem a strange statement but within the dream my father clearly needed me to understand he hadn't become a detective in his own life. He had never figured out who he really was; why he behaved the way he did; why he was angry at times; and what made him this way. He was sad about this and didn't want me to make the same mistake and repeat our family's patterns. I believe writing this book has given my father the vehicle to finally complete the cycle of his own consciousness.

We don't know what we don't know until we know and then we know! That's why I never feel shame in my discoveries, because the truth is, until I bring light into my own darkness I really don't know any better.

Our responsibility is to stop the patterns so our children don't have to carry the "sins of their fathers or mothers". We must live consciously, become aware, unashamed of our mistakes. The judgments of others and us are blocking the light from shining through, so please be kind, gentle, and don't judge what you discover. Judgment stops the evolution of consciousness.

Lynn Woodland from Namaste Publishing writes, "Blame and shame are disempowering, often immobilizing emotions that keep us unconscious and don't motivate us to be better people. They need to be tossed out altogether for the work we're doing here. Shifting from blame and shame to self-responsibility means looking at what you don't like about your life, not as something you did wrong (shame) or as something done to you by circumstances beyond your control (blame), but with the question, 'How does this situation show what I've learned to expect from life?'"

When my children left home, there wasn't a reason to live below the radar anymore. I believed it was safe to come out. There wasn't a need to protect anymore. Remember, this safety issue came from my own conditioning as a child. It has less to do with my own husband and family and much more to do with how and what I believed. This is very important because without awareness of our conditioning, we handle situations within our families from a distorted perspective. A perspective that isn't necessarily true; therefore, we risk continuing our parents' patterns. In other words, I raised my children as I was brought up (not on all counts) taking on the role of the protector and peacekeeper. You may think those as good qualities, but this wasn't honest because it kept the children and me believing we had to conform to get peace. This wasn't true; furthermore, it wasn't fair to my husband and it stopped us from being true to ourselves and then nobody wins.

Men never asked to be bullies and women never wanted to be victims. We don't have peace on earth and equality for women not because men want to remain in control, but because women haven't cultivated their inner courage to create the shift of humankind. It's my belief that this is what the world is waiting for. It's time we band together and find our inner strength.

The key is to do this with the utmost compassion for men. This isn't about tipping the scales and having the entire power shift to women. I believe that since women have been the peacekeepers for centuries within the families, we are capable of changing our world for the better - once we step into our own authentic selves.

We have the understanding and compassion required for this task, while having compassion for men who have also been conditioned and are conformed in their own ways. Women have been the primary care takers and their tendency to be enablers have prevented men from evolving. We haven't been honest about what we're really thinking. How many times have we heard our girlfriends say, "Yeah, I know, but he's really a sweet guy?" We forgive easily, we are compassionate: but enabling unconscious behaviour isn't okay. We can only help men by becoming our authentic selves. Men don't learn from being told, they learn by experience, which shows them if something is working out or not. Women are very different: We have a tendency to believe what people will tell us over our own truths. (When I refer to women and men I'm not necessarily talking about the male and female; within each relationship there is a dominant partner, sometimes it can be the male who is the more feminine) It's the balance of the feminine and masculine within each of us that we are trying to achieve, we do need both.

Hundreds of years ago witches were burned at the stake; female mystics had their heads chopped off because the men of that time didn't understand and were afraid of them. Therefore, it's understandable that women have been afraid of men's rules, strength, and power for centuries. However, in today's modern world we have rules in our Western countries that protect women so we don't need to be afraid any longer. Our fear is frozen in time; it's time to let it go. It's fear that gives another person power over us. We give our power away with the false belief we aren't equal to men and they have power over us. They don't believe it, but because we do, it becomes our reality.

As I mentioned in Chapter One, His Holiness the Dalai Lama has been quoted as saying, "It will be the women of the West that will change the world." I believe this is what he meant: Through awareness, we will shine light into our darkness and realize that we as women have been living our lives from a protection perspective, which hasn't led us to be clear communicators of the truth. We have enabled men by not speaking our truth. I believe when we start to communicate from our truth it will help us become our authentic selves and also help men to do the same. I believe this awareness will lead to a much more respectful and peaceful existence.

I'm aware I'm the only one who can give up my power. If I feel powerless, it's because I've shrunk back into my old fears and beliefs. I did what I did because I needed to feel safe, but I realize I don't need to do that anymore. It was a belief passed down to me. I know this is easier said than done, but I'm living proof. What used to be a matter of life and death for even speaking out of turn isn't the case any longer. The war on women is over, yet we are still fearful of confrontation. My sister said to me the other day that conflict creates intimacy; I really had to think about that. I think it's true, but as long as it's done with a compassionate heart. I discovered things about myself while in conflict; therefore, I was able to uncover some truths about myself. If only someone had told me that when I was in my twenties!

Men can't begin to understand what it's like being a woman. We're smaller, physically weaker, and mentally afraid from many centuries of being controlled. We don't need men to understand; that's not our job. What we need to do is join together as women around the world and collect courage from one another so we may climb out of old conditioning that doesn't serve us anymore. We must stop dealing with confrontation from our fearful selves. Our children are watching and we need to break this pattern. By our example, we need to give them the confidence to feel fear and go into it. I'm pretty sure God never made any rules based on male and female, so where did they come from? Man's fear of losing control.

As I see it, the difference between the roles of women as mothers and men as fathers and why women understand the greater good of all (not just for their own families) is something some men find difficult to understand. Maybe it's because they haven't physically delivered a child. This brings to mind the movie, *The Girl in the Café*, and a magical conversation when one of the characters asks the heroine why she was in prison. She replies: "Because I assaulted a man." When asked why, she replied: "Because he killed a child." When asked: "Was it your child?" She says: "Would it have made a difference if it was mine or not, it was a child." That line says so much about how women and mothers view the responsibility of protecting others. From my experience, women typically tend to stick together, while men act more competitively and are more separate from one another. So, who better than women (and feminine balanced men who understand this) to take this step to change our world for the greater good for all mankind? Women connect throughout the world; I believe men find it a lot harder to do this. Women search for consciousness because they have been dealing with so many more unselfish issues than men. This isn't a judgment about men because this has nothing to do with them. Change will only happen when we women stop believing in our conditioning.

Atrocities are still happening against women around the world; however, I believe as Western women set this new way of open and honest communication in motion (and step into our authentic selves) we can reach out to those countries where women still haven't any rights and help them step into their authentic selves. Once women do this, then men will have to follow and become their authentic selves and perhaps the world will live in peace, it's time for each one of us to take responsibility for ourselves and how we act.

From what I've witnessed, few people are truly happy or even healthy and this is largely because they are in conflict with themselves from their conditioning. It simply doesn't need to be this way. One of the main reasons I became so confused was because of my conditioning. I remember myself as a young girl, I was open, strong willed, much like a wild stallion: unstoppable. Once I got into a relationship, I began to act like my mother and I didn't rediscover my true self until my own children left home. I don't believe you need to wait. I just never realized I had put myself on hold for everyone else.

Last year I met a lovely local couple in their late twenties while travelling in Nepal. The husband's parents had chosen five girls and he was to pick one to be his wife. Happily, he picked a loving, beautiful wife and they seemed very much in love. Together they lived in the family house with their two-year-old daughter, his mother, his older brother and his brother's second wife. (His brother's first wife stayed in England to run her restaurant, so the mother decided her son needed another wife.) His mother governed the household. The child wasn't disciplined because grandma ruled. She said her son wasn't allowed to take his wife away for the weekend unless she said it was okay. One evening we were invited for dinner; the wife and sister-in-law cooked. While we ate with their husbands, the women ate in the kitchen. Our young Nepalese friend explained the ritual in which all the women of the house must praise him and kiss his feet in respect because he is the man of the house and is taking care of them. He said he didn't like that his wife had to do this, but his mother insisted that the tradition be continued.

The women who are continuing with these rituals are preventing themselves from becoming authentic. It's their conditioning and they don't even know they could break free from it. They are likely protecting their families, or at least they believe they are. The wife in this Nepalese family works with her husband in their business and is a big part of the office life, yet it seemed she is still considered "not equal" and not even by her husband but by the rules of the family: even in 2011. Throughout the world, women aren't seen as equal and worse they don't believe they are. It's still happening because of this belief. You can say it's cultural, but if we hold on to this belief, women in those countries will never be treated with the respect they deserve. We can't hide behind culture anymore; it's more about human rights than cultural beliefs. Language, food, music, and ceremonies are cultural, not female circumcision, rape, honour killings, child labour, or slavery.

Once women start believing they are equal to men, then men, based on this change in belief, will stop trying to control them. As I see it, it's this co-dependent relationship that needs to stop.

Let me share another story I heard when I was in Nepal: Thirteen-year-old girls were being sold for prostitution in Indian brothels. Who do you suppose makes those rules? Nepal seemed to me to be a beautiful country full of tiered gardens and farms, lovely people, and a gentle and humble existence. Yet because of poverty, they sometimes sell their daughters for what they think are nanny or housekeeping jobs across the border in India; just so the girls can send money home to their families. Of course, once these girls leave their homes in the mountains of Nepal, they are never seen or heard of again and their families never see any money. The girls go into the prostitution rings of India. When one thirteen-year-old girl realized what was expected of her, she refused, so they drugged her for three months, (a book called, *SOLD* details this girls journey). At the end of that time, she had been raped more than a thousand times. This isn't and never will be okay. Her story is brutal. I'm happy to say an American man rescued the girl and she was returned safely home to her family, albeit extremely damaged, as you can well imagine.

I believe brutality towards women in these countries will only stop when we as women join as one and band together and re-educate the world about what our modern-day role is - in the kindest way towards men so they understand without being afraid. Perhaps we should find a new word for "married". We could call it, "in our truths we unite," as marriage implies old beliefs, with old rules, and old expectations. We need a new ceremony for the new way.

As I see it, happiness and equality for all humankind: peaceful coexistence within our family unit and our world all begins at home. Individual consciousness is what will bring global consciousness and I believe Western women will lead the way.

Singer Kenny Loggins wrote a song with the lyrics: "Love should teach you joy not the imitation that your mommy and daddy tried to show you." Our children are watching us. If only we knew how they perceived us. Even if we don't have the awareness, they surely do.

Let's make it a conviction of the heart to become more aware so we don't pass our own pain bodies onto our children. From my point of view, our awareness and courage is needed to end the cycle.

CHAPTER FOUR

Did I Know Who My Mother Was?

❧

Song: "The Rose" by Bette Midler

My mom was forty when I came into the world; now there were eight of us. She would give birth to her last daughter, my younger sister, when she turned forty-three. I wonder, did she really want nine children? We were Catholics, so contraception wasn't allowed in my parents' world. I guess my mother didn't really have much choice, or at least she didn't think she did. How could she give her attention to so many people and still carve out a little time for herself? She couldn't have.

I only have two children and I can't imagine tending to the needs of nine and a husband.By the time I was old enough to understand or even care what went on in my mother's life, I was probably around eleven when we moved back to England. The little I remember about my mom, before the move, isn't very much. My eldest sister was married, had her own children and lived just around the corner from us in Tsawwassen. The next sister down from her was married and living in Australia with her three kids; sister number three was married with two kids and living in the next town. Each time one of my sisters got married and left home, it meant my mom had more to do. When the older girls were still home, at least they could help her out with the younger ones. We tend to remember the scary stuff more than the good; unfortunately, my earliest memory is when my mother was taken to the hospital in an ambulance.

For a few days she kept passing out. It turned out she had had a tubal pregnancy, a risky thing you can die from. I was so scared that she wasn't ever going to come home. I remember hiding behind the door to the rec room downstairs, peeking out just enough so I could see the ambulance attendants wheel her out the front door and take her away. I must have been about five or six by then. When Dad took us to visit her in the hospital, she opened the drawer beside her bed and it was full of chocolate bars, she let each one of us choose one. That was a real treat back then. Even in her illnesses, she thought of us first and put herself last. That's what moms do, certainly my mom, anyway.

My mother thought she could fix any problem we had with food or a sweet cup of tea. She was a great cook, particularly good at baking (scones were her specialty). I'm sure this is why all us girls like to eat and use food to make ourselves feel better. One autumn I was playing in the back garden and climbed up on the roof of the shed. I was determined to see if I could jump off the roof and land in a big pile of leaves on my behind - with my legs completely stretched out in front of me. Well, after several attempts I did it, but you guessed it, I knocked the wind out of myself. I couldn't breathe. I ran across the lawn, half bent over, trying to find a breath. Mom, as usual, was in the kitchen. She sat me down and began to make me a sweet cup of tea. The thing is: I couldn't breathe. The tea wasn't going to help, but she didn't know what else to do (I eventually caught my breath). She was horrible at dealing with our emergencies. It wasn't that she didn't care; it's just that it scared her when anything would happen to us.

I don't remember my mom doing much with me in the way of individual outings, she usually instructed one of my sisters to take me places or do things with me. Understandably, she had several to choose from and a large family to run. It was Nicky, sister number six, who took me to my little-league softball games and watched me play. It was just a block or two away, so we always walked there. I don't ever remember my mom or dad coming to watch any of my games; I'm not sure why. Too busy I guess.

I remember going off to ballet with two of my other sisters, Sharon and Andree. Mom would drive and drop us off, but I don't recall her ever watching us. I used to love doing interpretive dance at my ballet classes. I'd close my eyes and let the music take me to places in my imagination; it made me feel safe and free and happy. I know Mom made our tutus, the outfits for the performances we put on; she was really good at sewing. At school I remember getting the citizenship award for the five years I attended school in Canada. This was for the student who showed an all-around balance towards work, friends, and helping out the teacher, but I don't remember my parents being around for that either. It's strange, really. I'm sure other people must remember things their parents did for them while they were young, but I don't, at least not until we moved back to England when my dad taught me how to play the violin. I do recall when I stayed off school sick, my mother never made a fuss. It was always okay for me to stay home, even if I was faking it sometimes. She would get me colouring books and crayons and buy special Lucozade fizzy pops for me. It made me feel special and excited to have one-on-one time with her, which didn't happen very often. At one point, just to make ends meet, she even looked after another child - like we needed another girl around the house. She was the same age as my little sister and a playmate for her until she went off to school herself.

I don't remember my mother ever working outside the home when we lived in Canada, even when we kids were in school. And I haven't got a clue what she did while we were in school. I do recall one time, when I was about eight, I forgot my lunch and I was horribly embarrassed. I had this nasty teacher and she saw I that I didn't have my lunch so she made me stand at the front of the class till my mom got there. I was so humiliated. I hated any attention being drawn to myself, but I remember my mom brought me an awesome lunch that day in a brown paper bag: full of all those things that aren't good for you. She must have run out to the store, because the bag had a bottle of apple juice, a chocolate bar, a peanut butter-and-jam sandwich, and a wagon wheel. I loved it. It's funny how little things stick in your mind forever. The humiliation I felt that day has never left me.

We only had one car in those days. I don't remember how Dad got to work, likely on the bus. He worked as an engineer for CP Airlines, so he had to travel to Richmond every day. It was a big car, one of those American station wagons; after all, it needed to be able to carry eleven of us to church on Sunday mornings. One day when Mom had gone to get groceries as she pulled into the carport she hit the accelerator instead of the brake and the car went straight into the back of the workshop. She was so short, barely five feet tall, and she had such a hard time seeing out over the hood. Grocery shopping at our house was a big event, I'm sure it must have taken a few hours. Brown bags were coming out of that station wagon for an hour after she arrived home.

I'm starting to realize my mother was more like a manager than a mom. She must have been with all those people in the house, bills to pay, mouths to feed, kids to clothe. It always seemed her mind was elsewhere; perhaps she wondered where she had gone herself, was she doing what she wanted, or was she acting out of her conditioning? Had she just been a wife, had nine children, done what my dad or society wanted her or expected her to do, had she put herself on hold for us? She didn't have time for herself, how could she? I'm sure she was just coping the best way she knew how.

My mother taught me how to cope, but she didn't teach me how to stand up for myself. My parents didn't go out when we lived in Canada, but when we moved back to England they went to the pub every night. Even that time wasn't for her, there wasn't anyone there for her to chat with; she went because Dad wanted to go. He probably needed to get away from all of us, all that feminine energy!

What did my Mom do for herself, I wonder? Did she have her own friends to go out to lunch with? Did we have parties? I don't remember anything my mom did for herself, except maybe go to church, but then all of us went, so she didn't even get to do that on her own.

When we moved back to England, six girls lived in the house Dad built. We had one bathroom and three bedrooms. Mom and Dad got one bedroom and the rest of us shared the other two: three to a room. Mom used to escape to the bathroom, just to get some peace. This was the only place she could get a moment to herself.

I know she liked to cook; she liked to make preserves and jam. She loved roses and shared Dad's interest in gardening. Funny thing, when Dad died she seemed to lose interest in gardening. She sewed and knitted, but something tells me she did these out of necessity more than passion. It was cheaper to make things than to buy them. Much later, I learned she did like poetry, but what I remember most about my mom was she liked peace and would do anything to get it, sound familiar? I always knew she loved having her girls around her, even if she wasn't interacting with us directly and she had a great sense of humour. I loved to see her laugh, which seemed to bring out the real person living behind the mom mask. I'll never forget the time she was making stock with pig's trotters and before she put them into the pot she chased us girls around the house laughing her head off. We were laughing too, but freaked out at the same time. I jumped out the bay window onto the grass; it was at least a four-foot drop. She thought it was so funny she nearly wet herself. Sometimes I would wonder if my mom had lost it, particularly when she had this strange sense of humour. It was as though she were rebelling against all the things life wanted her to do, but she didn't want to do them. That was our mom and I loved her anyway.

It wouldn't be until much later in her life, when she and Dad moved back to Canada and after I was married, that Mom finally started to do things for herself. She was a wife, mother of nine and by the time my youngest sister left home she would have been sixty. As I see it, that's late to start remembering who you were as a girl and what your dreams were all those years ago.

My mom said her parents thought her sister was the brainy one who would go to university and she would be the one getting married and having children: And that's exactly what happened. My aunt never had any children so we never had any cousins: not like we needed any. My aunt had a nervous breakdown at a very young age and ended up in a mental institution. In those days, they treated people with shock treatment. It must have been awful; she wasn't ever the same after that. But here was our mom, coping with nine kids and running two businesses with our dad (They had a sweet shop back then and another business rewinding electrical components in London) it just goes to show that what parents project onto their kids can have a huge effect on them. My mother's parents didn't think she was smart enough to go to university, so neither did she. She believed them, though it was a lie. She was smart. She had an amazing ability to add up numbers in her head. For many years she had to run a household, for eleven people, on one income. She made dinners out of nothing and we never went hungry. That was her talent, making something out of nothing.

I have to say my mother seemed more comfortable in the sister role rather than the mother role. You would think that growing up in a house full of girls we would talk about all the necessary stuff, such as the birds and the bees and periods, but Mom never spoke about anything. In fact, one day when I came home from school with stomach cramps she sent one of my older sisters, Denise, to talk to me. I was sitting on the loo and Den sat on the side of the bathtub, she started telling me about periods and explaining what would happen and what I needed to do when it arrived. I remember thinking how she hated to have to explain all this to me; she wasn't comfortable with it herself. In fact, none of my sisters were. It was like a big secret. You would have thought by the time my turn came, they would have been more comfortable about talking about it - after all I was number eight. I swore if I had a daughter I wouldn't do that. Why was everyone so uncomfortable about this stuff? As it turned out, I didn't have my period after all. Poor Denise, she went through all that for nothing. That day I just had diarrhea, but now I knew what to expect.

So is that what happened to my mom? I wonder at the age of sixty, what did she think? Did she ever do what she wanted to in her life? Did she have aspirations for a career, a passion to go somewhere, to do something that was nothing to do with her husband or us girls? Even if she did want these things, did she ever believe she could just do them and be herself? After my father died, she came to my house for tea one afternoon and she talked about how she thought she was a healer and had wanted to try doing hands-on-healing. When I asked her why she didn't start, she said: "Because it's not really done in the church. God is the only one who can heal and it would be frowned upon." I told her God works through us and I encouraged her to try anyway, but to my knowledge she never did. She spent her life doing what Dad wanted and watching him do all the healing and connecting with people. She took the back seat. I'm not sure she even knew what she thought or what she wanted. She had spent most of her life thinking about everyone else and what they wanted, forgetting herself.

How many women get married, have a family, and never fulfill their own dreams? I knew from a very young age I wouldn't be one of those girls. It wasn't that I'm selfish, but I always had a sense of adventure and of being someone, standing on my own. I remember when I was thirteen years old; I thought I was the bee's knees! I would get myself all dressed up in my prettiest dress and go for a walk into the village, about five miles down our lane, imagining I was off to the big city. I felt so grown up and independent, no one was ever going to tell me what to do.

From my life experience, I've come to believe that worse than not being loved by another is not loving yourself enough to be who you are and thinking others are always more important. There is a belief that runs through our family, which obviously started with our mom and most likely came to her from her mom, to be true to myself will mean hurting someone else and I won't do that. So you compromise yourself for the love of another, believing this will sustain you. But one day, the resentment will start to grow and your ability to love will diminish. While you are living in resentment, it's very hard to love and yet you have decided this is what you have to do. We can change our beliefs about this chronic pattern. As I see it, only when we are true to ourselves and speak our truths can we really not hurt anyone else, even if it doesn't feel that way in the moment.

Consciousness, which is the road to peace, can't be born from trying to keep the peace through being dishonest. This isn't real or honest. Speaking your truth, which may create conflict, is the road to peace and intimacy. I learnt that from experience, it wasn't until I learned to express my truth to my husband that we could finally become intimate again. In expressing my truth I didn't feel resentful towards him because I knew everything I did and said was my choice. I couldn't blame him for them any longer. I don't use the word "intimate" lightly, or refer to a sexual event; to me what that word means is I have the ability to feel a connection to my husband on a much deeper level in which our souls are synchronized, as though we have travelled to a different reality together.

Looking back and realizing I had followed in my mother footsteps, primarily as a peacekeeper, I just wasn't happy. I was confused why others didn't want to keep the peace like me. Why did they cause such confrontation? Now I understand. To go against yourself just to keep the peace only harbours resentment and anger within you, it doesn't bring any light into the darkness. The fact is: it just keeps fuelling the dark. Being a peacekeeper the way my mom and I were was a result of our belief system and we were unaware of what this was causing. What my mother saw as protecting herself and her children against the wrath of my father was, in fact, keeping him the way he was. He never grew beyond whom he was because Mom's peace keeping held him in the same place. He didn't evolve. He didn't know any better. Because she enabled his bad behaviour, he never had to shine light into his own dark corners to ask himself why he behaved the way he did. This is what I mean when I say: "Women have stopped the evolution of men." This, of course, happens the other way around, too, when male peacekeepers do the same thing to their partners. It's not a gender thing, it's just that it happens predominately more with women than with men.

I don't want my words to be taken as a criticism or judgment, or for women to think we have done something wrong, because we haven't. I believe everything is happening as it should be; however, I feel it is time to make a shift into our next stage of evolution as women. By stepping into our authentic selves, becoming non-judgmental about what we are thinking, honest and transparent to our men and in all our relationships, we will be taking a huge leap forward in consciousness. Once we do this, conscious men will follow because their only other choice is to stay within their unconscious behaviours and continue the struggle to find unconditional love for themselves.

My mother and father loved each other deeply until the day they died. However, it's when I saw my father verbally abuse my mother that made me wonder how this could be love. He would say: "Shut up woman," if he wanted her to stop talking and shout at her with complete lack of respect. Oh, I know he didn't mean it. I saw this many times, but it didn't seem very kind to me. She would just take it because she was keeping the peace. That's the thing, you can say "I love you," but those are just words. It's how you treat someone that makes that person feel loved, not what you say. My dad treated my mother this way because he was unconscious. I'm sure he wanted things to be different, but he never delved into his own issues or got any help for them. He searched, but it seemed in all the wrong places. It reminds me of that saying, "You can't fix your problems with the same mind that created them." Did he want nine daughters and work all his life just to make ends meet? Did he buy the things he wanted for himself, or did all the money go to feeding and clothing the kids? Did he live his dreams? What I do know is that he never healed his own wounded ego from the hurts of the past and they became his triggers. How he responded to my mother and other people during those trigger moments came directly from past experiences. Perhaps if he had he worked on those, life would have become naturally more peaceful and fun for both of them.

I know he knows this now through my dreams. Did my mother deserve to be treated this way all her life? She loved my father and forgave him, but did she help him, herself or us kids by keeping the peace? No. It turns out that keeping the peace is just another form of control we learn growing up. I wish I'd known sooner, I most certainly wouldn't have tried.

My mom had lost respect for herself and she decided even if it wasn't okay how Dad spoke to her; she accepted this was who he was. She coped; knowing he didn't mean it. The trouble was, while she wasn't receiving any respect from him, we children grew up doing exactly the same thing. My dad didn't recognize this part of his own unconsciousness, perhaps had he done so, they would have achieved a mutual respect for each other and a much more peaceful, kind, loving relationship.

As I see it, women as peacekeepers are holding men back. They're keeping them in a place where they don't have to look into their own unconscious. As women we believe we are helping to maintain the peace for our children and ourselves: just as I did. I would like to make a note here, depending on the parent's personalities and who is the family nurturer that it could actually be the other way around in which the men are the ones keeping the peace in the house. In that case, they aren't helping those women to evolve either.

I want Trevor and I to live a full life: one in which we have mutual respect for each other and fulfill our dreams. I believe this is possible as this is exactly what we're working towards and will achieve.

Both our children are peacekeepers; it's a combination of their personalities and what they learnt from watching us. However, I'm helping them to see the truth. It's time for them to remember who they are without their conditioning. They don't like conflict or confrontation either, but I hope through my own journey of discovering what I did and why I did it that they, too, can learn from me that peacekeeping isn't the road to happiness. It's not honest and real; it's a band-aid and can't last because it's not truth. I want my children to have the freedom to express all of who they are and never to feel that they must stay small and hide to protect or compromise themselves for the love of another. For me, being your authentic self and allowing those around you to be the same is unconditional love and that's what I want for them.

If you're still not convinced happiness and health will effortlessly follow you (once you step into your authentic self) and allow those connected to you to be able to do the same, then I leave you with these extraordinary quotes written by two women. One woman had a near-death experience and the other, Grace, is a seventy-year-old dying woman.

Taken from the book *The Top Five Regrets of The Dying*, by Bronnie Ware:

Grace says, 'Don't you ever let anyone stop you doing what you want, Bronnie,' she said. 'Promise that to this dying woman, please.' I promised and went on to explain how I was fortunate to have an amazing mother who had taught me independence by example.

'Look at me now,' Grace continued. 'Dying. Dying! How can it be possible I have waited all of these years to be free and independent and now it is too late?' There was no denying this was a tragic situation and one that was going to be a constant reminder to live my own way.

In her bedroom, dotted with sentimental artifacts and photos of her family, we shared hours of conversations over those first weeks. Her decline was happening quite fast, though. Grace explained that she wasn't against marriage, not at all. She thought it could be a beautiful thing and a great opportunity to grow, through shared learning. What she was against was the doctrine of her generation, stating that you had to stay in a marriage regardless of anything. And so she had, all the while forfeiting her own happiness. She had dedicated her life to her husband, who had taken her love completely for granted.

Now that she was dying, she didn't care what people thought of her and anguished over why she hadn't worked this out sooner. Grace had kept up appearances and lived the way others expected her to, only now realizing the choice to do so had always been her own and was based on fear. Although I offered support, including the need to forgive herself, the fact that it was all now too late continued to overwhelm her.

The second quote is by Anita Moorjani in her book *Dying to Be Me*:

After being taken to hospital to die of cancer, she had a near-death experience and pronounced clinically dead, but she was given a choice to return to Earth to share what she learned about herself and the reason she got sick:

"Why did something so big like this terminal cancer thing happen to me just for not realizing my own magnificence? Simultaneously, I had this understanding: Ooh, I see-it didn't happen to me, because in truth, I'm never a victim. The cancer is just my own unexpressed power and energy! It turned inward against my body, rather than outward. I knew it wasn't a punishment or anything like that. It was just my own force expressing itself as cancer because I didn't allow it to manifest as the magnificent, powerful force of Anita. I was aware that I had a choice as to whether I wanted to come back into my body or go onward into death. The cancer would no longer be there because the energy was no longer expressing itself that way but was going to be present as my infinite self.

Always remember not to give your power away - instead, get in touch with your own magnificence. The only universal solution I have is to love your self unconditionally and be yourself fearlessly! This is the most important lesson I learned from my NDE, and I honestly feel that if I'd always known this, I never would have gotten cancer in the first place."

Anita's message is we're only here to realize we're not who we thought we were. We're so much more. It's our soul job in life to step into our authentic selves, that's why we get sick. It's to propel us into meeting the challenge of being ourselves and live our truths.

CHAPTER FIVE

Family Conditionings

⤜⤜⤜

Song: "Do What You Have To Do" by Sarah McLachlan

Even if I didn't know it back then, I began to witness myself in the summer of 2002 when I put several discs out in my back. I turned forty that year and I remember trying to do some work in the garden and how impossible and painful that was and I asked myself: How did I get here? How did I not listen to my body until it finally shut me down? I had always been so sure of myself: successful and courageous. Life was easy for me, but I found myself in a situation I hadn't ever been before: not in control. Much later, I would see this as my first, "Ah ha" moment. I was caught off guard and sent into a whirlwind of uncertainty.

Even then, I believed our bodies shut us down when we don't listen to them, so I wondered why this had come about. I knew I had done something to piss my body off. A friend lent me a book on back injuries called, *Healing Back Pain* by John Sarno. As I worked my way through the chapters it became apparent to me that back injuries were related to family issues.

So, I took the time and reflected on what was going on in my own family and around me.

It started to make sense. My daughter and niece, who are the same age, had just entered high school. My niece started experimenting in all sorts of ways, as teenagers do and I was frightened for her. She reminded me of myself as a young girl and I knew what I got up to. I felt as though I was being tortured because I couldn't do or say anything to stop it.

The word torture is interesting. "Torture is the act of inflicting severe pain (whether physical or psychological as a means of punishment," according to Wikipedia.

Why was I being punished? The thought of torture made me think of restriction, not being able to move; hence, I thought of my back.

My mind said, *She* (my niece) needs help, but conflicting with this was the belief "I shouldn't interfere in the family affairs of others". It was like being mute, screaming to be heard, yet nothing coming out. She was in trouble and I felt helpless: this helplessness sent me over the top and contributed to my back problems.

Over the next couple of weeks I finally pushed past my belief I shouldn't interfere and tried to alert my niece's parents, but they didn't think anything was wrong. I even tried to tell my other sisters, but to no avail. They just thought I was jealous, though jealous of what? I couldn't make sense of it, so once again I felt unheard and still scared for my niece. Or was I scared for me and not being in control? Was I, in fact, just in my own fear?

Due to the mental torture and the fact I couldn't get anyone to help me, my niece, or have any understanding of what was happening; my body shut down one morning after a coughing fit in bed. I realized I had done something serious to my back. I couldn't stand up straight.

I tried all kinds of therapy and living on anti-inflammatory drugs (two years later these were taken off the shelves because they were causing heart attacks). I took painkillers that I mixed with the anti- inflammatories, which then caused me to have a stomach ulcer. I wore a portable tens machine, which stimulates the muscles and takes your mind off pain 24/7, yes even to bed to appease the pain. Finally, I went to the doctor again and he referred me to a specialist. I had an MRI, which confirmed there were actually three discs with problems. Then, I was given the option to go for surgery, but I wasn't ready to be cut open. For anyone who has had a disc problem, you know what it feels like. It's a dreadful groaning of lower back pain that never eases off, like being in childbirth, or having rotten period pains. It takes you down and puts you on edge.

I walked slightly hunched over, but I still went to work full time. Yes, I'm a trooper, I'm a woman. I spent a lot of money and time going to the chiropractor, physiotherapist, naturopathic doctors, and acupuncturists: until one day two years later I'd had enough of being a victim of this pain. I wanted out. I took all my pills and flushed them down the toilet. Then I picked up the phone and hired a personal trainer. This was the beginning of my healing. My trainer was fabulous. She didn't doubt that my back could be healed; her confidence meant so much to me. I remember going to my first session when I couldn't even pick up a piece of tissue off the floor. I wondered what had I done to myself and what was I supposed to learn from all this?

My trainer lent me a book called, *Lick the Sugar Habit*. Yes, you get the picture. Books have been an important part of my evolution and most often offered answers to my situations in the moments when I needed them. My trainer told me about a guy, who reads your eyes, so I invited him to the house. My husband wasn't convinced about all this alternative stuff at that time, but he encouraged me to give it a whirl; thus, this iridologist came to the house to do a reading on me. He told me I was close to a nervous breakdown and if I didn't stop eating sugar, worrying about things outside of my control, and start taking better care of myself I would be going down. He could really read all this in my eyes? I thought, Wow. First the book, *Lick the Sugar Habit*, now this guy is telling me to stop eating sugar. Hmmm, there must be a message here for me. He also commented on the concussion

I suffered from many years ago. I had forgotten about it, but it left me with a bald spot on my head; thanks to my sister swinging me around by my feet when I was little and my head catching the corner of the coffee table. How could he know that ... I thought I better listen up and take heed, since I knew I couldn't continue worrying about things outside my control. I was damaging my body by my mental suffering, not to mention abandoning my own family by spending time trying to help my niece. What message was that giving them? But why was this so hard for me?

Shortly after the iridologist's visit I decided I had to change my beliefs about this situation - but it was difficult. I had to step away from my niece's troubles and take care of myself first. I had let myself get so caught up in her world I had abandoned my own. This required me to become quiet and go inward. I spent very little time outside of my own immediate family while protecting myself and watching how I unfolded. It was like there was a "me" acting out my life and a "me" watching me act out my life, two of us. Well, this is true, because one part of us is running unconsciously, so we can be acting unconsciously and consciously watching ourselves, which makes us conscious. I know that's confusing, but stay with me. Once you see what your unconsciousness is doing and why, you refrain from doing it anymore and you never go back, it's just not possible. For example, when you learn to read, you can't unlearn this skill. It's the same thing with consciousness. You learn to change the way you look at things and handle them. It's the wounded ego that doesn't want you to find this out because it is afraid to change.

This realization has led me to continue on my journey of unravelling "me" while being in this conscious state.

For the following two years I became very quiet and private. I only went to family events when I had to. I went off all sugar products of any kind, which was difficult, but clearly good for me. I started to notice things changing about myself: physically and mentally. My mind became clearer; I didn't feel my eyes wanting to close in the afternoons at work. My nails and hair grew faster, I lost weight, my normally dry and rough elbows became soft and smooth. I stopped having hypoglycaemic moments during the day. Before I quit sugar, I would feel this intense need to eat something when I woke up in the morning, around ten o'clock and later around three o'clock in the afternoon. I wasn't hungry, it was an anxious feeling that my body was calling for something to make it feel calm. Once I was off sugar, all of that went away. I visited my naturopath monthly to check on my blood work, my progress, worked on my new diet, workout routines, and started taking care of my own immediate family.

The most difficult thing for me was work. We ran a family business in which two brothers had married two sisters and started a company together. That all worked fine, until the situation with my niece. My partners in business were also my niece's parents, so that meant every day I went to work I might be faced with discussions about their daughter. I couldn't talk to them about it because we didn't see things the same way. They obviously thought I was wrong. Given I had made a pact with myself to not discuss her anymore with anyone (because I couldn't do anything for her and couldn't get them to listen to me) to save myself from further destruction, I had to refrain from talking about her. To make matters worse, my own daughter and son would come home and tell me what was happening at their school and parties. I learned to listen and left it at that. For me, it was like being in a bad relationship and not being able to get out. I knew that whatever I heard I had to *let go*. These little words became paramount in my new belief system.

One day, after finding myself in a bookstore, I walked past a shelf and was surprised when a book fell on the floor. I looked down at the book and around to see if anyone else saw it fall. I picked the book up and read the title, *Co-dependence No More*. Then, I read the back of the book and thought, that's weird, this is about alcohol addiction and not something I'm interested in, so I put it back on the shelf. Later, at home, I looked up the word co-dependence.

Wikipedia says: "Co-dependency (or co-dependence, co-narcissism or inverted narcissism) is unhealthy love and a tendency to behave in overly passive or excessively caretaking ways that negatively impact one's relationships and quality of life. It also often involves placing a lower priority on one's own needs, while being excessively preoccupied with the needs of others. Co-dependency can occur in any type of relationship, including family, work, friendship, and also romantic, peer or community relationships."

I thought, oh, perhaps that book was meant for me after all, this was a sign for sure, so I went back to the store and bought the book. Reading chapter after chapter I thought, this isn't for me, it's boring and about alcoholics, none of which I'm interested in. But then I came to the middle of the book and saw three pages that repeated the words, "Let go and let god". *Hello, I think someone is trying to tell you something.* I'm not sure if I picked up that book today whether it would have those words on those three pages, but that's what I remembered. This was a colossal message meant for me. Letting go was exactly what I had to do in this situation. I had to trust I was getting in the way of whatever was going on in the lives of my nieces and sisters and I had to step away, no matter what. I had to accept this was their journey, not mine. That's faith.

Still, I thought I'd give it one last shot with my sister and I asked her to see a therapist with me to sort this out. She emailed back a no. It was interesting how I felt about her response. My adult self said, I understand and she probably thinks I need to get this stuff done on my own and I'm sure she thinks this is being respectful. The child in me said, she doesn't want to be my friend. Did this mean she doesn't care enough to try to work this out?

Then I jumped in my car and what song should come on the radio but Sarah McLachlan's *Do What You Have To Do*. This was another sign for me to let go for good. The words: "I don't know how to let you go" brought tears to me. I realized I simply didn't know how to let go of my sister. Then I asked myself, why don't I have any problems letting my kids do their thing? I never worry; I trust I have given them good tools to face whatever they need to in life. I asked myself again, why is this so hard for me? Then, as I was painting that day and accepting the fact my sister said no, I suddenly felt the "let go". I felt as though she had given me permission to let go of her and the responsibility of making sure she was safe. In saying no, she was saying she was okay now and ready to go it alone. It clarified my problem: I was afraid to let her go because somewhere along our young lives I believed I needed to take care of her and her daughter. I wonder where that belief came from - obviously, my mother and my conditioning.

I often talk to people about my family and they see our lives as complicated and confusing from what I tell them, yet somehow I never saw it that way. My family, like many others, was only just on the normal side of dysfunctional. Perhaps I was in denial most of my childhood and lived in my own bubble. I grew up in a family of nine girls, and I *do* remember my mother telling me to watch out for my sister in school and on the bus. One time, when I was about twelve years old and my hair was really long, there was an incident on the bus with a boy and my sister. I got into a full-fledged fight with the boy and he was pulling my hair (I never liked my hair being pulled) and it sent me into an immediate rage. We both ended up getting thrown off the bus that day. My sister was two years older than me, but much smaller and daintier, plus she almost died as a baby from whooping cough. Therefore, somewhere in my belief system was the belief that she couldn't take care of herself. It didn't help that my dad drank too much and too often and created some scary moments in our young lives. As a result, I suppose there were times when my sisters and I retreated to the safety and comfort of one another.

I decided it was time for me to seek out a therapist, since I still had some unanswered questions about our relationship. I remember thinking I had to pick someone cleverer than me since I knew how my mind worked. I really wanted someone who was going to be straight and help me through this. I wanted the truth about me. During the session, the therapist told me it was expected and understandable that I would take on the responsibility of my sister and my niece because growing up in such a large family we had become totally enmeshed. I didn't have a clue what this word meant, but fortunately she gave me a sheet of paper that explained it.

I learnt that we become enmeshed when we don't learn personal boundaries within our families. It's when we see "loving" as fusing of our egos with theirs, as in the enmeshed "family ego". This kind of fusion doesn't respect each individual's right to be themself. The therapist told me our upbringing and personal history determines our beliefs about our own boundaries and growing up in a large family it would be quite typical for me to be experiencing enmeshment. She also stated that having a father who drank and a mother with few boundaries created the perfect mix for a co-dependent relationship. She said under these circumstances, it would be understandable for me to have taken on the role of taking care of my siblings, especially with my personality type. She told me I had to stop taking care of people; such as sisters and nieces because I was getting in the way of their own journeys and I wasn't being helpful. I was being an enabler. I didn't like to hear that. I knew what that word meant.

I told the therapist there was always a part of me that didn't want to take care of anyone anyway. That was the real me speaking, but then there was this voice that said, I was helping and if I didn't help out, it meant I was selfish and a bad person. Talk about confusing. How was I supposed to figure out which voice to listen to?

These words swished around in my head many times before I could finally quiet the voice that told me not helping was selfish;

and believe by actually doing nothing, I was being much more respectful and helpful. Once again, I proved to myself that what I believed was causing me this grief; to the point where I had let it harm my mental and physical states.

I must be a quick learner because I only went to the therapist once. At the end of our session, she asked: "Do you think you need to come back for a second visit?" I remember saying: "Nope, I think I got it figured out, thank you very much," and that was that. As I drove home, I couldn't believe how wonderful it felt to be told I wasn't a horrible person for not "helping" and how free this made me feel.

Can you see the magnitude of damage we do to ourselves and each other from our beliefs? I almost lost a sister, a niece, my health, and god knows what else by my actions and not even because I wanted to. I believed I was a horrible person if I didn't help. I have come to see there are some children who believe everything their parents tell them and then there are kids who rebel. I must have been one of those kids who believed. I'm glad I figured it out before I brainwashed my own kids. I'm happy to say both of them: "Know you can't help anyone. You can support someone, but you can't know what is better for that person. It's their job alone and by honouring that, you offer respect and love. Each one of us is on our own journey."

I did change my beliefs and everything worked out brilliantly. My sister and niece went for counselling and worked through their issues together and my back finally settled down through the work I did with my personal trainer, my beliefs, and change in diet. Today I don't have any problems with my back at all.

This didn't happen quickly. It was a process that took at least four years before I could actually say my back was healed.

Throughout this challenging time with my niece and sister, my mother would call me up to make sure I was "taking care" of things: whatever that meant. I could feel she was agitated by what was happening with my niece. To communicate with my mother was to "go around the houses". She never was very clear, so it left you guessing what it was she really wanted you to do.

Part of my obsession in trying to help my niece was definitely increased by my own mother's fears. One afternoon, there had been an incident at school with one of my niece's friends and I wanted to speak with this young lady to help her out, so she and her mother came to my home. Everything was going along fine. The talk I wanted to give this young girl was about sex and contraception. I had heard she was leaving herself open to being violated and not protecting herself from getting pregnant. The talk all went well and her mother clearly appreciated it, as did she, until my mother phoned. I excused myself to talk to her because at this time she was frantic about my niece and I didn't want her to worry and make herself sick. She sounded so terrified on the phone that something bad was going to happen to my niece, this triggered my own fears, and when I returned to this girl and her mother, I was in a state of anger and fear and I blurted out: "That was my mother, she is frantic about my niece. If anything happens to my mother, mark my words, you will be at her funeral." Of course, as soon as those words left my lips, I wished they hadn't. My intentions for this young girl were all good and until my mother phoned, all was fine. You see, because of my mother's fears, which heightened my own; I became "unconscious" and in doing so said some very unkind, unthoughtful, unnecessary words to this little girl. Well, as karma would have it, only a week later my mother choked on a piece of food, complications set in, and she passed away. I shouldn't have said what I said that day but I did and I couldn't take it back. I, of course, don't blame myself for what I did. I know it was wrong, but it showed me that through my own fears I had become unconscious and in doing so I had hurt others and it wasn't okay. My poor mom lived most of her life in fear of something: much later I would realize why.

A few months later, I caught up with this young lady and her mother and apologized for what I had said. They appreciated it, for they felt bad too. My mother had passed away and they were understanding. This was hard for me for two reasons: I had become so unconscious as to be malicious and because my mother had passed away. Life's lessons can be so harsh.

Before she died, as my mother lay in the ambulance on the ferry (enroute to Victoria's city hospital) I sat with her. She was so calm, which wasn't like her at all. She asked for a drink of water, which an attendant gave her. Later, we would find out she had a collapsed lung. When she first choked, my sister took her to our small, local hospital and the surgeon tried to dislodge the obstruction in her throat. However, he accidently poked a hole in her esophagus, which meant all the food and drink was entering into her chest cavity: which had collapsed her lung. Once we got her settled at the city hospital, I remember the doctors told us the problem was with her heart, but it wasn't. Three surgeons approached her bed and told her what had happened and that she had a twenty percent chance of surviving an operation. They said if she had come to see them the day the incident happened, instead of four days later, her survival rate would have been much better and how sorry they were. I couldn't believe what I was hearing. Were they saying my mother was going to die? You have to have known my mother to know how she was after being told this kind of information. It was so strange. She was always such a chicken and scared about things, especially hospitals. She had had a bad knee for years, but wouldn't have it operated on because she believed she wouldn't wake up from the anaesthesia. Not this time. She was calm and content. She handed me her wedding ring, cross and chain, then said: "Don't worry Chenty, if I come back and you're standing here that will be fine, but if I see Dad [who had passed away three years earlier] then that will be fine, too. It's in God's hands now." She so missed my father.

As they wheeled my mother away from me, it felt like our umbilical cord had been cut. I felt such a deep grief that we were being separated for the first time: perhaps forever. She told me she was sorry she shouted at me earlier that week and that she had bought me a card to say she was sorry and was anxious for me to find it in her car. I assured her I would look for it.

After they took her to surgery, I went to the pay phone to call all my sisters. I told them to pray like they never had before because the odds weren't good. Our mom only lasted a few days after the operation. The surgeon said it was like trying to repair a wet tissue, every time he tried to stitch her throat, it would tear apart again. As she lay in intensive care, the doctors informed us they found cancer in her right breast. They said she likely knew about it but didn't want to tell any of us. It was horrible to watch her with a tube down her throat and in so much discomfort.

A day after her surgery, her surgeon told us she had caught an infection and the stitching wasn't holding. They would have to operate again and try to make a new throat from her stomach: she would never be able to eat real food again. She would only be able to take liquids and she would likely be in hospital recovering for six months. He said to us: "As your mother's surgeon, what would your mother want me to do?" Oh my God. I sat there among my other eight sisters thinking about what Mom had said to me just before going into surgery. She was calm and didn't really care what happened to her; either way, she said would be fine. I knew if I told him that, he would let her go and that would be that. Oh how I didn't want to tell him.

I felt anxious: no one else knew what she had told me. If I didn't tell him, no one else would know either, but could I live with myself knowing that was her wish? What if she survived the second operation and spent the rest of her life being mad at me because I didn't want to let her go? She was so calm and happy when she said what she wanted. I decided I had to tell him, knowing what the outcome would likely be, but it was her wish. He thanked me for the information and the decision was made to make her comfortable, but to leave her condition in God's hands and see what the night brought.

That night I slept in the lounge of the special care unit along with my sisters. I drifted in and out of sleep and I could hear them chatting and reflecting as I woke up to a vision of my father standing at my feet at the end of the couch I was sleeping on. I knew he had come for Mom. He looked like he'd just woken up, his hair was sticking up, but I got the sense he was here to check up on all of us. He just wanted to make sure we were okay and for us to know Mom would be with him again. I'm convinced he also showed himself to me so I could comfort my sisters. In the early hours of the morning, I think it was around five o'clock, my youngest sister and I woke up at the same time just seconds before the nurse came in to tell us our mother had passed away. You can imagine nine girls standing around her bedside. I hadn't been there for my Dad's passing, so this hit me pretty hard. She was gone. I remember sitting on the hospital floor holding her hand and crying. I had a sense her spirit was still in the room and she was looking back at us knowing she was exactly where she wanted to be. A sense of calm came over me and I knew I had made the right choice in sharing her wishes with the surgeon.

Days later, as I checked through my mother's car, I found the card she wrote to me. It was so sweet, with a picture of a little girl hiding behind a tree, smiling and she wrote:

Just a note Chenty to say how sorry I am about yesterday. The only excuse I have is that I have been feeling really low just recently, but I should not have taken it out on you!! It's hard when you love people, maybe too much, and I suppose this is the first big hurt since Cy died, not having him around to say, 'sit down, I'll make a cup of tea.' I'll not mention this again. God Bless much love mum xxx.

Tears ran down my face, sadness came over me and I felt her drift away. She was gone and these would be the last words she would ever write to me. She loved my father dearly. They had a bond beyond bond. They had worked through so many difficult things in their lives together and certainly during the last fifteen years, I could see they finally figured things out between them.

It's a very strange feeling when both your parents pass away. They have been there for you your whole life and when both of them are gone you feel like an orphan. In difficult times my parents were always there for me and now where would I turn for help? I knew that if I ever needed them, I could just go to them and they would stop everything to tend to my needs. Wow, that says a lot about who they both were to me: they loved me unconditionally.

Three months after my mother's death, I remember watching a movie that wasn't even relevant to her or death and something came over me and I just heaved with tears. This final letting go of my mom hit me out of the blue. It was a final exit of the pain from losing her which I was now ready and able to let go of.

CHAPTER SIX

Seeing Through New Eyes

⤠

Song: "Listen" by Beyonce from the film "Dream Girls"

In early 2008 my husband's father passed away. He was from England where we both grew up so we decided to make a trip back to pay our respects and reconnect with his family. I thought this would be a trip for Trevor and I would enjoy the ride, but this was not meant to be. To my surprise, this was a trip for and about me.

Years ago a psychic had told me I would be visiting England; yet at the time I couldn't think of any reason why I would want to go back. I should have known, eventually it would make sense. So off we went to hang out with his family and swing by his dad's gravesite to pay our respects. When his dad died, Trevor didn't feel anything. Perhaps going back would trigger something within him for it seemed he needed to connect with his family. There wasn't a lot of love between him and his dad. He was a typical English father who believed in all the old-fashioned ways of bringing up children: a heavy hand, a strict voice, little or no communication, and certainly no compassion. I had met him when Trevor and I started dating. I never liked him or trusted him and I think the feeling was mutual. Their two personalities clashed; there was always confrontation. I was his girlfriend, so I was in the line of fire too. I remember many times how he would try to hurt me just to get to Trevor. He would say unkind things such as: "Who cut your hair? A grass cutter." He would embarrass me about not wearing a petticoat (who wears those now?) under my homemade skirts, because apparently you could see through it. I was young and sensitive and didn't like being in his presence. He was unhappy and that made him mean and grumpy most of the time. My sister dated Trevor's younger brother, now that was different. They were the golden couple in his dad's eyes, which made it even worse for both of us. At the time *Dallas* was on television and his dad compared us to the couples in that drama series. We were the unpopular low-lifes and my sister and his brother were put on a pedestal. It was plain to see his brother was the type of guy who knew how to stay out of his father's way, while Trevor on the other hand wasn't diplomatic. He said what he thought, which was a problem in his dad's eyes. There was just so much conflict: I hated it.

We arrived and went to stay at our friends, Nigel and Rose's, house. It had been years since I had been in England and I saw things with new eyes. It started off subtle, this new vision of mine, seeing things from a new perspective. Nigel and Trevor have been best friends since they were sixteen-years-old, but they hadn't seen each other for twenty years. Nigel was the best man at our wedding and although we moved to Canada, we had stayed in touch with them all this time. As a young adult Trevor would head over to Nigel and Rose's house to retreat from the anger and confusion of his own father and to get "girl" advice, so they were in his life long before I was. While we were there, Nigel suggested we take a motorcycle trip to Europe with another friend of theirs. Nigel made all the arrangements, from booking hotels to which route we would take. We were to go for seven days.

The first night at Nigel's house was already different from other times. I went to bed early, which I never did normally, for no specific reason. I remember Trevor sat up for hours chatting with Nigel and Rose about their lives and what they wanted to do next: including coming to live in Canada. Normally, I'm in on those conversations, but I just didn't feel the need that night. So I was starting to become aware of changes in my patterns. The next day, we were going over our route and figuring out what we still needed to do before leaving. I just sat back and watched as Trevor and Nigel chatted up a storm about the upcoming trip, their lives since they'd seen each other last, and listened to their laughter. It was nice to see them like that together. They really reconnected and I could see in that moment they unconditionally loved each other, more than brothers really. I hadn't ever seen this between Trevor and anyone else before, so this was another awareness new for me. In the past I had seen these two together only briefly and I guess I never noticed it back then, but now it was different or perhaps I was different. I really believe this was the key: something inside me had changed. It's as though I was in a new dimension of being really aware, with a heightened sensitivity to my surroundings, yet an observer as opposed to a participating perspective. I discovered this allowed me to stand down. By that I mean I realized Trevor now felt safe and I could relax. He and Nigel felt like two people beating to the same drum. In myself I witnessed I had been standing guard and protecting him from being hurt, why I didn't really know.

Trevor and I met in the small English village where we both lived. I was fifteen at the time and he was twenty and engaged to be married. I was just completing high school and he was already a qualified machine fitter, had a full-time job, car, apartment, and well on his way to having a family life. We were introduced through horses. One of my sisters had bought a young colt and she and I would spend hours together in the field with the horse. We loved this time together; it was truly a bond between us. She decided to go back to Canada and so I was left with the horse. By that time I was trying to break him in, but I was too afraid. I knew Trevor's mother had horses of her own and asked her to help me. She decided this was a job for her crazy son, who was known to stand on the backs of horses while riding our local beaches with his arms reaching fearlessly up to the sky. She brought him to meet me and help out with my horse. He now tells the story of when he gave me a leg up to get on the horse's back, that was it: he was smitten. I felt he was a funny and charming guy. One thing led to another and before long he had called off his engagement and we started dating. I was attracted to his deep-blue eyes, his charm, his endless energy, his excitement for life and his little red-and-white mini! Funnily enough, I was too young to feel any guilt towards the poor bride to be, isn't youth wonderful? Anyway, it's no wonder I felt the need to protect him. There were times when he came unexpected to my house in tears and angry about how his father had treated him and other family members. One time he came by and his fist was bleeding: he had smashed a wall. It would have been his dad's face otherwise. I just assumed it was my job to rescue and protect him. What did I know? I was only fifteen.

Looking back, I see I am a rescuer by nature. I like peace in my world. I don't like confrontation and conflict, so it upset me to see him like this. His dad seemed to spend most of his life angry and grumpy and that played out into his family. After spending four years watching his family life and its drama, I decided I needed to take care of him. Isn't it funny how relationships often start this way? One feeling the need to rescue the other? I grew up in a Catholic family of nine girls; therefore, I didn't see any physical violence in my own world, which is why this probably bothered me so much.

While organizing the bike trip to Europe, Trevor felt good, relaxed, and happy. I sensed he was safe and in good hands. I just went with it; I was fascinated to watch Nigel's and his relationship unfold. I noticed things about Trevor that were never as clear to me throughout our twenty-seven-year marriage as on that day. One was how compulsive he was with his new toy, a GPS. He wouldn't leave it alone. Nigel was trying to show him how to use it and he was getting frustrated with him for not leaving the buttons alone. I watched how my husband was without my interference. He wasn't different, but I was detached from his behaviour, so I could observe how he acted. I know this might seem obvious, but to me this was a new concept. This observing was another step in seeing with new eyes from a completely "detached" prospective. Yes, I had observed him before with people but from an "attached" perspective in which I was protecting. It's very different and this understanding has made such a huge change in my own life.

As the day wore on, I began to see how compulsive Trevor was about things. Before this, I never really saw it as a condition, but put it down to how he was. I realized, in other words, the way he acted had nothing to do with me. In fact, it wasn't about me. That was such a revelation. I had seen for the first time in our relationship that how he behaves is who he is, part of his makeup, and it's not based on anything to do with me. I had become detached, no longer tethered to his emotions or actions. I also realized I wasn't only attached to what and how he behaved for the protection of himself, but how he would treat others. I thought it was my job to soften the blow, so to speak. It was never about "what" he said as much as "how" he said it that upset people.

After a couple of days of recovering from jet lag, we arranged to pick up our motorcycle from the rental place which was a two-hour drive from where Nigel lived. Our plan was to ride from England and through seven other countries (in Europe) all in a week. It should have been obvious to me then that this trip wasn't going to be exactly what I'd wanted to do. The guy who rented the bike to us said to my husband: "Now just be careful 'cause when you open up the throttle it will go like hell, the front end may lift up, and you may lose her off the back."

You can imagine my face and thoughts when he said that. I held onto that thought for the whole trip and it definitely played a part in what was to come.

The first leg of the journey was a bit scary, but I survived the M25 motorway and all the traffic filtering into London with only a few tears - which I kept to myself. We had never "filtered" between the traffic before, since this is not allowed in Canada (I still didn't know if we were breaking the law driving this way) so that put my nerves on edge to say the least. The traffic was horrendous. I was terrified that someone would open a car door as we passed between the cars and we would be knocked off the bike.

At Dover we got on a boat, crossed the English Channel and embarked upon the continent from Calais, France. A few days later, when we were going through the Swiss Alps the Italian truckers were driving so crazy that I became anxious. The speeds at which they travel at on the European motorways are crazy compared to those in Canada. I started to realize this was definitely a guys' biker trip; we hardly stopped to eat along the way (only coffee and a croissants) which is never good for my digestive system and me. It seemed all we were coming across in Europe was espressos and bread. We never even stopped to shop: not even window shop. I guess my idea of a trip to Europe was different from theirs. The scenery was beautiful and the weather was great, but it wasn't quite what I had in mind. The trip sounded romantic when it was explained to me, but what can I say, the guys organized it.

Travelling through Switzerland was beautiful. We started to climb up this steep, windy road, with a view looking out over a valley: stunning. I noticed my husband's energy suddenly change and it felt like he was in the "groove," determined to get past these crazy Italian drivers. To me he seemed like a cat when it's on a mission to catch a mouse, so focused in that moment, as though he had no idea I was still on the back of the bike. Had he forgotten I was there? Then there was that moment of "opening up the throttle," (you know, the one I mentioned earlier when the rental guy told him to be careful or he would have me off the back). Trevor took off, overtook the truckers, and zoomed up the mountainside, around the hairpin bends, and towards our final destination for the night. The more we rode, the more terrified I was. I was hot, sweating, hungry, and scared. Why, oh why, didn't I say something? What was wrong with me?

On several occasions I'd been hypo-glycemic, so with my anxiety building that feeling was getting worse. It must have been 30 Celsius that day and I was wearing my black, (complete-with-liners) biking gear which only attracted the sun further, so I was hotter than hell and anxious: all this was fuelling my hypoglycaemia and creating even more anxiety within me.

In the centre of my fear, I asked myself, how can I get off this bike? I want to get off. It's strange I didn't talk to Trevor as we both had our bike-to-bike communication units turned on in the helmet, but for some reason I didn't tell him to stop. I think it was because I was afraid I'd break his concentration and we'd crash, so I just stayed silent and terrified the whole ride: frozen in fear.

My mind said, we just can't stop and get off as we are in the middle of Switzerland and in the Swiss Alps. There isn't much around, we have to get to our next stop for the night. Our friends and this guy we didn't know very well were with us and I never liked to make a fuss. I pretty much went along with anything and everything, but this time I just couldn't. I was done and my body was telling me NO. All I kept thinking was, how can I go on with this fear? And, I was very aware of this conversation with myself; it was kind of surreal.

I thought, I know … when we stop I could have a nervous breakdown, that will work. How will that look? Then another voice in my head said, no, that's what my sisters did when they weren't considered or nobody heard them. No, I'm not doing that, I am going to be heard! I wasn't in control of this bike and Trevor was riding like a madman. I was terrified and it wasn't okay. A moment of calm came over me, we were still going a million miles a minute on the back of that bike, but I asked myself, where have I felt like this before? The voice inside me said, sailing. I thought, Yeah, that's true. When we crossed the ocean at night and there were storms, I was terrified. We sailed the Caribbean for three years, for three months at a time and when I had my night watch being so far away from shore in the darkness terrified me. Again, I had a feeling of being afraid without any control. I thought, no, not this time, he's going to listen to me, I'm afraid and it's not okay.

All this time I was also thinking how interesting that I was having a conversation with myself while being so terrified. I was asking myself questions and getting the answers right away. There was a part of me that wasn't frightened at all; it was the one with all the answers, the "wiser self" if you like. Then, there was the terrified part that didn't know what to do. I was starting to become fascinated by this experience and myself. Are there two of me?

By the time we stopped at the next gas station, I had peaked. When I got off the bike, my legs could hardly keep me upright. I stood up in front of Trevor and pounded on his chest. I was enraged, saying he was a "Fucking bully". I didn't even take my helmet off, that ride had exhausted my adrenals and my fight or flight response had come to my rescue. Trevor had no idea that I was terrified that whole time. He'd had a great ride. He was completely oblivious to how I was feeling. He was looking at me like I was nuts; he really didn't have a clue.

I sat on the curb and Nigel came up to me, bumped his helmet against mine, and asked if I was okay. I burst into tears again and said: "No." I screamed through my helmet and called Trevor a bully again and stressed that he hadn't considered me and I was angry and exhausted. Nigel called Rose to come over to "deal" with me as I took off my helmet and sobbed. My husband still had no idea what was wrong with me. I had been pushed further than my body was prepared to go. He apologized, but for what, he still didn't really know. He said we would go slower and continued on, heading towards the hotel. I got back on the bike without speaking to him and we rode slower. Now I could relax a bit and reflect on my actions. It seemed I had crossed over a barrier and there was no turning back; it felt good and I felt strong. I thought if this place we`re headed to for the night doesn't have a kitchen or it's shut, I'll demand they open it for me because I needed to eat. My body had gone through an extreme adrenal exhaustion and food would help stabilize me. This new, demanding me wasn't whom I was used to being.

When you're hypo-glycemic, your personality changes because your body needs a sugar fix. It's just like being an addict. I had moved into a part of my psyche where it seemed my mind wasn't any longer in charge of my actions, because its choices were ones my body didn't agree with. I had put "us" in danger, so the body spoke. There are times in our lives when our minds clearly don't know what's best for us, our bodies take over and shut down just to finally be heard.

Wow, why didn't I listen to myself? Why was it so hard for me to ask for what I needed?

In my current state of finally "speaking my truth," I felt empowered and I was going to be heard and get what I wanted. This was so out of character for me, because normally I wouldn't have said anything that night and just gone to bed mad. I never would have caused a scene in front of our friends.

Five hours after my meltdown fortunately for me and everyone else the kitchen was still serving when we arrived at our hotel. At the dinner table I told everyone what had happened to me in great detail (including my thought process) and I didn't care what anyone thought, even my husband. I was fascinated by myself and the thoughts that had been flowing through my head. It was so liberating losing my governor, the part of me that says what's right and wrong. I felt as though I had found my voice and myself, it was exhilarating and exciting. I must admit the group just let me rant on while nodding and smiling like I was off my rocker. We decided to take an extra day off from riding allowing me to regain my strength. As we rested in this quaint village nestled in the Swiss Alps, I continued in this new state of being; clearly stating exactly what I wanted and didn't want with the personality of a spoilt child. The group said very little and let me be. I think they were worried I was having a nervous breakdown, and hey I'm pretty sure I was, but it felt *gooood.*

The next day, the guys wanted to go up the mountain on the gondola and I just couldn't. The thought of putting my body through any more stress was unbearable. I was pretty sure I was all out of adrenals for now, so I said: "No." My husband wasn't used to me saying "No". He then tried, as he always had, to convince me it would be fun and that this was what I wanted to do. "Not this time," I replied. My "No" had a very different tone to it. My voice was so strong and deep, like some elder had been summoned forward from the depths of my being to answer for me. Nigel noticed I was indeed different and got my husband to drop the issue and together they went up the mountain. Rose stayed behind with me and we sat on a rock together. She was very sweet. She could see I was fragile, but she also sensed a strength in me at the same time. She said she admired me because I was so strong and confident, hmmmm, that's not what I was thinking. I was still wondering why the hell I said "yes" when I meant "no", like, what's with that? Why didn't I stick up for myself and ask for what I needed?

Feeling a little stronger in my body and still aware I was in an empowered state of being, the next day we continued on to our next stopover. We found a great little place to stay for the night and once showered and unpacked we headed to the pub for a drink before dinner. We all ordered giant pitchers of beer and relaxed into telling stories, laughing, and enjoying the moment. Well, I don't know if the oversized beer pitcher had anything to do with it, but that night there was a moment in which I noticed myself become very dominant with Trevor and it made me sad because I really wasn't being kind and I knew it. I had become the bully who was bullied. I had to make a choice. Did I want to stay in this state or not? I knew I didn't. It wasn't really who I was and I realized I just needed to let my husband know I wasn't prepared to be pushed to those extremes anymore: he had to start considering and hearing me. This brings me back to the song at the beginning of this chapter in which Beyonce sings, "You should have listened". So I decided I didn't need to be a bully to get what I needed, I just needed to ask and be honest about how I was feeling and to start sticking up for myself and believing that what I want does matter.

This was like another form of seeing with new eyes. I had been put in a situation in which the polite me had to step aside. I was in a fight for my life and I had to do what I needed to survive.

For the rest of the trip I felt like a princess. Everyone seemed to be concerned about me and how I was feeling: including my husband. I guess I had achieved what I had unconsciously set out to do. In spite of my mind trying to control things, my body stepped up to the plate and took over. When we got back to Nigel and Rose's house in England, the guys wanted to continue riding for a few days down to Newcastle. Rose had to work, so I decided to stay put in their home and let the guys go for their ride on their own. I wasn't ready to endure any more adventures and instead decided to rest, read, and relax. I wanted to reflect on what I had gone through.

Thank God for moments like these because this was the beginning of my new life and the new me, or perhaps the rediscovered me. Perhaps this is what's meant in the phrase ``It's time to remember the truths, we have been conditioned to believe in the lies."

From that day on, I had an awareness of my true self: courageous and strong yet kind and gentle, a sense of my own compass, a well rooted tree not to be blown over by the storms.

I had changed; I was speaking my own truth, what a beautiful thing. Looking back, I can't believe I didn't do this before. Why did it seem so impossible in the past? My body stepped in to bring awareness that I wasn't sticking up for myself and we (my mind and my body) were in danger.

I am now detached from my husband's behaviours. I realized all these years I had been rescuing him from his pain, his words, and his relationships: everything. I had been catching him before he ever hit the ground, at his expense and mine. He never asked me to, it was perhaps because he never felt secure and safe and I thought it was my job to fix that. Well, it wasn't; furthermore, I had become an enabler. I wasn't doing any good at all. I was a rescuer and not being respectful of him and his journey. But more importantly, I had got in the way of his growth. Pain leads to a new level of consciousness. When you stop someone else's pain; for example, I interfered with his journey. I stopped him from being able to reach his authentic self. It's funny, because if I were to tell a guy this story about me on the bike he would say: "Why didn't she just tell him to stop?" If I were to tell a girl this story she would say: "Why didn't he consider her?" Neither reply is wrong; our expectations of each other are different. When it comes to the balance of feminine and masculine within each one of us, this analogy is just a small example of how we think differently and perhaps it's time to reach out into each of our opposite sides to come to understand ourselves and each other better, it's all about balance.

It was summer when we got back to Canada and shortly after our return we headed out on our sailboat for the weekend. I was different now, I'd changed, I knew it and so did he. I was happy I'd found my voice, but I could tell Trevor was having a hard time with the new me. I wasn't quite as agreeable about things as I used to be; I actually had an opinion, ones that didn't necessarily match his anymore.

I remember being in the dinghy and going down the inlet at

Samson Narrows near Butchart Gardens when a sailboat passed by. Trevor said hi to the person at the helm, but the guy was kind of snotty and his response wasn't very friendly. I noticed Trevor's energy change and he said something harsh to the guy. There it was again, this energy I didn't like being around and now it seemed even more pronounced than before. In my new state of consciousness, that I had stepped into in Europe, it now seemed impossible for me to be in the presence of this energy. It wasn't who Trevor was, so where did it come from? How can someone switch so quickly from being calm to being angry? What triggered it? I was so confused.

On our way back to the boat, Trevor mentioned he was still feeling strange about not having felt anything when his dad died and he thought that perhaps he should see someone about it. Shortly after this, we both booked in to see a therapist. We met the therapist and I mentioned how Trevor had spoken to this boater, so then, of course, the therapist started on about anger and his father. Then, to my surprise, somehow I started talking and what came out of my mouth was what obviously needed to be said and witnessed: it was all about how I had been protecting Trevor from himself all these years and how I was too tired to do it anymore. I couldn't believe what I was saying. Even though it was easy for me to say the truth, there was another part of me thinking … God, I can't believe you were doing that all this time, who do you think you are? There you have it, unconsciousness. At the end of my blurb, I felt bad, because Trevor really didn't even get to talk much about his dad, it turned out to be all about me and what I needed. After that we went for lunch and he was so sweet, he didn't have any idea how much energy I had been putting into watching over him and why did I do it?

I realized I never had to do this; it was just what I did. Then, I set out to figure out why I took this role on in the first place.

Growing up in a family of nine girls, we were always covering or rescuing one another, dodging around our father's behaviour so we could all live in peace. I guess I just did the same with Trevor as I had done all those years at home with my sisters; the thing is I never knew I was doing it before.

Since my experience on the motorcycle, I feel free to speak and do what I've come here to do without a voice in my head telling me otherwise. There isn't a governor filtering my words anymore. My new commitment is to speak my truth, no matter what. My new mantra is to be honest and vulnerable. Perhaps it never felt safe before. I was afraid to have a voice and to ask for what I needed. My beliefs had led me to a life of, I don't matter. I`m sure the Catholic, turn-the-other-cheek philosophy played a big part in that belief.

A note about speaking your truth: Remember, it's just that "your truth" be aware of how you present it. If you want to say: "Please don't shout at me," perhaps change it to: "When you shout at me it makes me feel afraid and I end up not saying what I really want because I`m afraid you`ll get mad and shout more."

I now believe we all have a time to go through the door and this was mine. Because this was such a profound life-changing experience, I want to share it and other stories with all of you. It is my hope that in my own small way my experiences will help shine some light for others, bring clarity about why we do what we do. Consciousness is now my passion. It's the ability to observe oneself in all situations and stand back to come to an understanding that there is always a bigger picture. In Europe I was thrown into fear: the strongest fear of all in which I was afraid for my life. In that moment I became the "observer of me": what that felt like and how I had everything I needed to solve my own problems. We humans are truly amazing. Now, I observe everything differently - people, nature, and the world. My eyes have been opened.

Believe it: the truth will set you free.

CHAPTER SEVEN

Discovering the Wounds

꧁

Song: "Forgiveness" by Sarah McLachlan

In the fall of 2009 I was weeding in the garden one Saturday afternoon and every time I went to stand up my right side cramped up. It felt strange; it came as fast as it went and since I had never felt anything like it before I wasn't sure what it was. A voice in my head told me to stop and go inside, but I'm stubborn and wanted to get the weeding done, so I kept on working. My mind drifted and the strangest thoughts arose from nowhere about my husband and one of my sisters: along with the word "shame". At first I thought they had done something without telling me and were ashamed, but then I got this wasn't the case. What came to me was that they both felt shame and it had to do with me. Finally, I gave into the voice in my head. I quit weeding and I went inside. I still felt a bit weird but didn't make too much of it.

That night I went to go for a pee before going to bed and noticed my urine was red. Yikes, that scared me. This had never happened to me before. Trevor was already in bed, so I drove to the hospital and sure enough I had a kidney infection and was put on antibiotics. I went back home, but couldn't go to bed as I had to keep drinking water to flush out my kidneys. I was peeing constantly, so I decided to stay up and read. The book was on

Sekhem energy, which originated from Egypt and is thought to be the purest of healing energy systems (I had taken a workshop about it earlier that year). The book stated: "Kidney problems are related to fear, criticism, and disappointments. Kidney stones are just solid lumps of fear. Fear to do with relationships is the predominating ones but fear of all events." I wondered what this could mean. What was I holding onto and afraid of facing?

There was a poem about forgiveness in this little book, so I decided to read it out loud to myself even though I hadn't yet identified what my fear or anger was about, other than the obvious, which was "fear to be myself". Given I'd been thinking about Trevor and my sister in the garden earlier that day I held them in my thoughts and took that as a sign. I've come to know signs are everywhere. There is a higher intelligence at work. You can call it guardian angels, God, universal truth; call it whatever you want, but know we are being helped in this life. We just need to have faith, open our eyes and heart and we will see the signs.

The writer, Sekhem Master Helen Belot, who now lives in Australia and is working on healing the planet, she instructs you to do the following:

> Prepare a special place (outside or inside) and make sure you have at least an hour of quality time. If inside, burn candles, incense, etc. and play some of your favorite quiet music.
>
> Take a sheet of paper and write down all the names of people who have hurt you, made you angry, frustrated or upset you. Also note down why or how.
>
> Don't forget to include yourself.
>
> Imagine all these people gathered around you, and when they are all present (including yourself) speak the following words to them.
>
> Imagine them listening and reacting with a smile, thanking you and leaving quietly.

Forgiveness

I do not know why
You did what you did
And I do not know why
You said what you said
I do not know why
You are the way you are
But I accept that is where
You need to be just now
And I forgive you, and
I forgive myself

I release all anger, bitterness and resentment
Past and Present
And I forgive you, and
I forgive myself
And I release both of us
In my love

And so be it

I now easily release all resistance
The past has no power over me
I am the only person that thinks in my mind
My mind is powerful
I now choose thoughts that free me
I trust myself to release and let go
I am powerful and safe and secure
I am free…I forgive everyone
I forgive myself…I forgive the past
And by doing so…I am free
I am free…I am free

I FORGIVE EVERYONE
I FORGIVE MYSELF
I FORGIVE ALL PAST EXPERIENCES

FORGIVING EVERYONE...FORGIVING MYSELF

I AM FREE... I AM FREE.

I followed the above instructions and finally went off to bed.

It turned out to be a strange week full of events that would enlighten me. A couple of days later Trevor and I went out for dinner with friends. I had put on a favourite scarf, a blue one with flowers and created a triangle that sat across my chest, but Trevor didn't like it and wanted me to take it off. He had always been very verbal about what he liked and didn't like me to wear. In the past I would change just to keep the peace, but the new, speak-my-truth me didn't want to be told what to wear anymore, so I expressed myself. This wasn't because I'd become stubborn; it was about expressing my true self through my choice in clothes. I've learnt the thing about coming into your power and speaking your truth is that you have to keep checking in with yourself about whether it's your ego that wants to win, or simply your truth. You'll know because you will feel different. When the ego is triggered, you will feel fear and anger; when you're speaking from your true self, you will feel calm and peaceful.

Trevor was adamant about the scarf. I told him I would take it off at dinner to get him off my case, but I didn't. When we got in the car to go home that night, he was mad and said I had lied to him about taking the scarf off. I find it interesting that he saw this as a lie because in my mind it wasn't. I had simply forgotten about the incident and hadn't thought about the scarf again until he brought it up on the way home. That night his anger towards this silly incident bothered me. It wasn't like him to be so mad and adamant about things like that and I wondered what this was all about. I was honestly surprised at how intense he was.

The next morning, I told him I didn't like how he was on my case about the stupid scarf and that it spoiled our night. I told him he must be angry about something else and he needed to get some help to figure out why he was so mad at me. I left it at that. By this time, I had realized that how he reacted usually had less to do with me and more to do with things within his own beliefs: beliefs that I couldn't have possibly known about. My ability to detach from him helped me understand that I was just the trigger.

Until that time Trevor had only been to a therapist to discuss his dad dying. Most men hate going to therapists; they don't like to talk about their emotions. In the past, any time I mentioned therapy it was clear he didn't want to go. For the first twenty-five years of our marriage, we really never argued and this was primarily because of who I was then and what I believed. Life was good and I hadn't had the awareness about other things; such as why I said yes when I wanted to say no. At that time in our marriage, I accepted this as the way it had to be. Therefore, sex was the only issue that constantly arose between us back then. He wanted it all the time and I didn't. He would go on about it and get angry until I folded and gave in. That was my old nature and pattern. The odd time I stuck to my guns and would suggest we see a therapist about it, but then he would back off and agree he had a high sex drive. This went on for most of our marriage; it was the only thing we argued about. Now, all of these incidents were happening around the same time, likely because I had stepped into myself and this was unsettling for him. He couldn't follow or read me anymore: he didn't have control. I had changed and it made him extremely uncomfortable.

It was Thanksgiving that same week and our daughter was back home and living with us. I had invited our son, his wife, my sister, and my mother-in-law for dinner and I was really looking forward to it, but everything seemed to go wrong that day. Our new oven wasn't working properly to cook the friggin' turkey so dinner was delayed. Trevor was testy and getting on our daughter's case; for example, we were watching an old video and he was teasing her about her weight in it (which she was already self-conscious about); nagging her about leaving her backpack in the hallway; and just generally being negative and unkind. It seemed the more of me I exposed; the crankier he got and nagged at the kids - which only confirmed why I conformed. Our son's wife wasn't doing well. She was pale and thin and had to leave the dinner table early to be taken home by our son. I'm very intuitive and I got a strange feeling about her that day. It seemed she had just gone through some kind of trauma, but she didn't say what it was and I couldn't figure it out. Of course I didn't ask, but it was clear something was going on. All in all I had a lousy Thanksgiving dinner, in fact, it had upset me so much I wish I hadn't bothered. However, it made me realize I had to change something in my life. I couldn't go on witnessing such events without speaking out.

That night, as I lay in bed trying to get to sleep, I started to think about my daughter-in-law. Since I was a child I have prayed every night before falling to sleep. It's just something I have always done, having been brought up a Catholic. That night I asked for God to watch over my daughter-in-law and help with her struggles. This got me thinking about my relationships and all the strange events of that week, my kidney infection, my forgiveness poem, and the scarf incident. As I fell to sleep, I asked for help to come in my dreams.

I dream and when I wake up I can remember and reconnect to my dreams. In fact, I don't like to be woken up before seven o'clock, since I'm not finished dreaming. Trevor wakes up at about six o'clock so he thinks I should too. Even when I wake at seven, I am analyzing my dreams as this process helps me to figure things out. It's what I've always done and I enjoy it. It's not that I'm not a morning person. I'm not cranky; I just like to finish processing before I step into the day. For most of my life Trevor has woken me up before seven and this has actually helped me to reconnect with my dreams, it meant I could fall asleep again to finish them, so I have to thank him for that. Anyway, in the middle of that night, I woke myself up realizing I had been crying in my sleep. As I lay there, I asked myself:

Why am I crying? The answer: Because you are being punished. I am? So I asked: What for?

The answer: For abandoning people.

I continued: Who?

Trevor, and three sisters." The names came to me and I asked: What are they punishing me for? Something I don't know I've done?

The voice in my head said: Trevor for breaking his heart when I split up with him when I was sixteen; my sister for my relationship with Dad and not being at his funeral; and another sister for seemingly choosing her daughter over her; and maybe even my youngest sister, too; or was it when I dated Trevor which meant I left her alone at home by herself?

I started to cry when the voice said they're punishing me. I felt so sad for myself, but it made so much sense to me, especially with my husband. I lay there reflecting on the past and thinking back to when we first met and those times. I hadn't had any relationships before him, how could I? I was only fifteen. I remember being a brat, stroppy, and strong willed. Trevor was head over heels for me, smitten for sure. I could get him to do anything for me; in fact, this was part of my problem with him and why I broke off our relationship. I didn't like who I was with him. So yes, I did break up with him when I was sixteen, but could he still be punishing me from all that time ago? We had now been married for twenty-eight years. How sad, I thought, and then drifted off to sleep, feeling quite wounded.

When I got up the following morning Trevor was in the bathroom brushing his teeth. I went up to him and looked into his eyes and asked: "Are you still punishing me for me leaving you and breaking your heart when I was sixteen?" His eyes welled up with tears. I had obviously caught him completely off guard. What did he know of my dreams and my answers? He didn't have a clue that I had had this revelation during the night. As I watched his big blue eyes swell up with tears, in that instant I knew it was true: He hadn't forgiven me for something I had done all those years ago. His wound hadn't healed. I looked into his eyes again and said: "Will you forgive me for breaking your heart all those years ago?" To my surprise, he couldn't speak. I continued: "You can't forgive me even though I married you and we have been together for twenty-eight years?" I was shocked, and thought what now? It's funny because I realized that even he had not identified this within our relationship. It was something hidden very deep in his heart.

We made coffee and climbed into the hot tub. I moved close to Trevor and asked him once more: "Will you forgive me for breaking your heart?" Again, he couldn't speak. I could see this wound ran deep. He had tucked his heart away never to be broken again. Sarah McLachlan has a line in her song *Forgiveness* that says: "You asked for forgiveness, you're asking too much, I have sheltered my heart in a place you can't touch, I don't believe when you tell me that your love is real." This song explains how my husband must have felt for so many years. He could never trust me with his heart or at least he didn't believe he could, so he kept it locked away. On some level, I knew this, because when we first met his heart was open. At that time I wasn't ready for my heart to be taken at such a young age, but the block in our relationship made so much sense to me now. Before, neither of us could express what it was. If the cause of our troubles hadn't come to me in a dream, I don't know if it would have ever been exposed and things may have ended up quite differently for us - and this was just the beginning. Reciting that poem about forgiveness seemed to release deep wounds from within both of us. I believe in forgiveness, even if we don't know why or what for. It affects the emotional side of us and forgiveness also has a profound physical effect. I can't explain other than to say our emotional state directly affects our physical state. I believe that once the emotional is healed, our physical can follow just as quickly.

You may wonder, given I'd broken up with Trevor, how we finally got married. It was because he changed; he realized that if he stayed true to himself he might lose me because at that time I was so young, independent, and strong willed. I was trying to figure out who I was and what I wanted. I was a kid, but he was five years older. To hook me, he knew he had to change. He had to become tougher, stronger, and seemingly more confident.

We weren't going out at his twenty-first birthday party, but he was dancing with another girl so you guessed it, I got jealous and made my move. Somehow we ended up with each other at the end of the night and the rest is this story. Trevor changed to catch me. He locked his heart away to become whom he thought I wanted him to be and in regards to what was happening now, perhaps it was time for his heart to trust again.

Trevor heard Jan Arden sing a new song that day called, *Broken* and told me that I had broken him. I felt sad for him, because I was such a bitch back then, he felt he had to change and protect his fragile heart forever. I felt punished for just being a child; I was too young to enter into the life of a full-time relationship.

Perhaps the kidney infection triggered all of those events to surface in my own consciousness, because they were ready to be healed once and for all. Being a detective in my own life has helped me to figure out so many of my unconscious behaviors and the key to this is asking. Even if you don't know whom you are asking, ask the trees, ask the air, ask in your dreams, but please ask. I could have seen the events in my life as just events: People get sick, have dreams, etc., etc., but I wanted to know why. It's my soul urging me to ask and become a detective in my own life. I believe peace can exist between two people and that both can live and be respected for exactly who they are. We don't have to compromise ourselves for the love of another. And it's because I believe this that I seek it so. It's like when you know there's a treasure to be found, so you simply won't give up until it's discovered.

Thanksgiving brought everything to a head. My body couldn't take it anymore. Even though the day and the meal weren't that big of an event, I couldn't stand by and be married to someone who couldn't see how his words were cutting and hurtful. It wasn't who I was; I strived to be kind to everyone and it hurt me every time Trevor was harsh to others. The more I tried to explain this to him, the angrier he got. At that time he just couldn't see it from another's perspective.

The following morning, during breakfast, I felt numb and tired and I was drifting in my own thoughts. I got in the car to drive to work but instead headed to a sister's house. As I walked in on her, poor thing she was just getting out of the shower, I went down the stairs to where she was standing and as she came out of the bathroom I burst into tears. Then my energy turned into an ugly rage. I smashed the walls with my fist, screaming at the top of my lungs that I just couldn't go on being present when Trevor was being unkind without being able to stop it. This was too painful for me: I had to get away. My sister was great. She didn't try to rescue or stop me. She just let me scream and when I was finished, she hugged me and said, "You need to get away for a few days," adding that she'd tell Trevor. So without even returning home to get my stuff, I caught the ferry and headed up Vancouver Island to where I didn't know and it didn't matter. I loved driving my car and listening to music. I felt calm and I ended up at a resort near Parksville, which was perfect; it was quiet, calm, and on the ocean. I booked myself in for a massage and just surrendered to the moment. As I walked back to my room, I remember thinking how I wanted to jump into the ocean to cleanse me, even though it was freezing given that it was October. I wanted to feel the ice-cold water and shock myself into realizing I wasn't the same person I'd been portraying myself to be. I'd changed and I wanted the cold water to wash any residue of my old conforming personality off my body. Then, I thought I'd shave my head too. This would let people know that I wasn't the same and I didn't want to be treated the same either. I was different. Okay, so both those thoughts lasted for about fifteen minutes and then I chickened out on both accounts, but I did think they were interesting possibilities.

From what I've witnessed, we're so afraid to be ourselves. We trap ourselves with false beliefs worrying about what people would do or say if we changed, so we don't.

Trevor was furious with me. He went into the fear of being abandoned: his issue with me. I had now done (or so he thought) what he was most afraid of. In my own mind I hadn't abandoned him; I was tired and needed some time to myself. He phoned me nine times that night and it wasn't pleasant. I felt bad for him, but I needed to save myself first. I knew our daughter was home with him and that my sister was going to see him and explain why I needed to get away.

I didn't sleep very much that night. I worried about both of us and woke up from my sleep thinking Trevor was already in the room standing beside me. I was afraid, but I did what I needed to do. He simply never understood how and what he said to other people affected me. It was never an outright fight between us. His energy was so strong I could hardly bare it sometimes. It seemed as though his anger was trapped within him he wasn't even aware of it, but others could feel it, especially the kids and I. I believe it was his fears, which projected outwards as anger that we were feeling from him.

The next day I drove home. It was dark when I arrived back and Trevor was sitting in the loft upstairs. I felt bad for having caused him so much pain, but I needed some time to myself. I sat on his lap and we held each other, then we got up and went for a walk in the dark. I was nervous at that point because he hadn't said much, so I didn't know what he was really thinking. Finally, he said: "You left me," and I knew he was referring back when I was sixteen again, so I knew I was dealing with this same issue.

I realized, through all of these crazy events of my life with him, was that his wound was abandonment. I thought I had created that wound, but as you will learn in chapter nine, I wasn't the first person to abandon him. I was just a compounding effect, which was controlling his behavior and our inability to get past it in our lives.

We're lucky to have a couple of close friends who understand our issues; they were both there for us when we needed them. One day our friend called Trevor and said he needed to see him, which was so unusual because when we got together it was always with the four of us. When my husband returned from that visit, he told me: "Ouch, that felt like he stuck a knife through my chest!" I thought oh, oh, and asked: "What happened?" Trevor replied: "He told me the way I have treated you and the kids sometimes wasn't okay. He said I was disrespectful towards you at times and I needed to get some help with my anger and wanted to know why I was so angry." He said: "You can't tell me anything I don't already know because I myself have been in therapy for years, so don't even bother trying, it's you, you have anger issues and it's not fair to take them out on your family." Our friend gave him an excellent little tip when he said: "Try treating your wife and kids with the same respect you treat mine." Trevor never forgot that; it was the best advice and message our friend could have given him.

I, of course, felt validated. Finally, someone other than me had brought his attention to the issue. I had been trying in my own way to tell him, but he just couldn't see it from my perspective. I'm truly grateful for the courage of our friend because it made such a difference in our lives. I'm also grateful to my husband for accepting his words with the intention from which they were given, from a place of healing and non-judgment.

That very week Trevor did as his friend suggested and booked an appointment to see a therapist. I also booked in to see a therapist, the same one I had consulted when I was struggling with my niece and sister. When Trevor came home from his appointment, he said they discussed how to manage his anger and the therapist had given him some tools to use to double check himself. He then asked me what my therapist said and I replied: "Nothing really." He was confused by my answer. I could see he was thinking she must have told me something, but in fact she said: "When he is acting out of anger, just keep bringing his attention to it." To do that required me to step into my courage and confront his energy that I so desperately wanted to ignore in hope that it would just go away, but as I was to find out, it didn't. It would take more than my courage to resolve the issue.

CHAPTER EIGHT

Ego and Illness

Song: "Faith of the Heart" by Rod Stewart

We don't need to get sick before we can wake up and be happy. How many times have you heard that phrase or that everything happens for a reason? Well, yes it does, but if I were to tell you that if you're sick, overweight, underweight, or just plain miserable and it's not necessary, wouldn't you be intrigued to find out why and how? There are people in the world who know this to be true and I'd like to share.

I believe we get sick because we are in conflict with ourselves. Our true self is saying: "You're not being true to yourself" and our wounded ego is saying: "No one is letting me be true to myself." Do you see the difference? One comes from a place of power and the other comes from a place of disempowerment. We're not being heard and we don't have the tools to get people to hear us; we're tired and frustrated and we don't know how to get what we need. We don't know how to communicate; we're afraid so we get sick, depressed or remain just plain unhappy. Sadly, this happens to children too.

Take a moment to sit quietly and write down what your heart really wants: right now in this moment to feel happy and at peace. When you have your list, imagine yourself communicating what's on it to those who need to hear you. How does that make you feel? Chances are, you feel afraid. This is the problem. How do you get past the fear to speak your truth?

The first step is to start taking care of you. If you don't know what that means, I'm about to introduce you to yourself. It's likely that you have been operating in this lifetime from a protective, conforming perspective. Step One is to find out who you really are and what you really believe.

It was difficult for me to get back in touch with my true self. I was filled with questions and doubts, which exhausted me to the point where I was just simply too tired and it all seemed so complicated. As I watched my son go through a painful divorce, I realized I had finally hit bottom. This was definitely my point of decision-making and I knew I needed help. My massage therapist gave me a book called, *Adrenal Fatigue* by Dr. James L. Wilson and after reading it I decided this was what was wrong with me. The book explains exactly what you need to do (and not do) to help your adrenals rebuild which I followed, but it wasn't easy. One of the biggest messages I learned was only you can help you get better.

Adrenals are responsible for so many functions and I believe their dysfunction is a pre-empt to mental illness. No, I'm not a doctor of any kind, but after experiencing this for myself, I can tell you it all made sense to me. The places my mind travelled during that time of health challenges were anything but stable or rational and there were occasions when I scared myself. I even thought, I'll get cancer, then they will listen to me, give me a break and I won't have to fight or defend myself anymore. I'll be left alone to heal and figure myself out. They won't question me, they'll just let me be and I'll do what I need to do. It seemed cancer had the ultimate answer for I believed when someone gets this disease everyone around them backs off, because now they know that person is in a fight for his or her life and this scares them to death. So much so, that everyone now just allows that person to do and be whatever he or she needs to, which is pretty extreme, but sadly too often true.

The thing about me; I have always trusted my intuition so I seldom wanted to see a doctor. I knew all he would do is medicate me and I wanted to feel everything. I didn't want to run away from my feelings; I wanted to wake up. There was an intelligence within me that must have known this was required. Basically, when you have to deal with trauma in your life, your adrenals pump adrenaline into your system to help stabilize you. If you have several traumas then guess what? Your adrenals don't have anything left to give. Your body takes from other areas and this depletes you of the essential minerals and nutrients you need and when this happens, your brain doesn't function properly and you get depressed. If that's left undiscovered and untreated, then more serious illnesses can follow.

I believe adrenal fatigue is an acute, under-diagnosed problem in our society today. The trauma doesn't have to be dramatic; it can be as simple as an argument with someone. Being a caregiver can also cause adrenal fatigue, so the events don't have to be hugely dramatic which is why I think adrenal fatigue goes undiagnosed so often. It can also come about from physical trauma to the body. This happens anytime the body thinks it's being attacked; the adrenals will respond automatically. Basically, the body has been in a fight or flight alert for far too long and far too often.

We need to understand our body talks to us and we need to learn how to listen to it. Illness is the purest form of consciousness. If you're ill, I believe, it's your body screaming at you to be heard. Ask yourself: "What am I not listening to that my body is trying to get me to hear?"

Speaking of listening, what I discovered about myself through all of this was that I wanted everyone else to listen and leave me alone. Then I could heal and I couldn't understand why they couldn't just do that for me, was that too much to ask? My husband was the hardest on me. He didn't understand what I was going through, it scared him and he just wanted to fix it and make it go away so I could get back to being normal. Normal is another interesting word; which normal, what is normal? I believe I let myself get to this stage because I didn't like what I'd become. I wasn't being true to myself, I wasn't being the real me. I was conforming. I wanted to cry on everyone's shoulder and say everyone was mean to me and I didn't understand why. I'd become a victim, but what I discovered was that "I" was not listening to me.

My son was in the midst of his divorce and the torture I felt inside had gotten the better of me, it had taken its final hold on me. At that time we were completing construction on our house and our dear friends loaned us their cottage. One day I was standing alone, looking out the window at the forest; the sheep were grazing in the field, the rabbits and chickens were wandering the driveway, and it was a peaceful sanctuary. I remember the moment, which came over me like a cloud and I wanted to give in, give up. It all seemed too hard, too much work, too sad. I was tired of thinking and over-thinking. I just felt like I didn't even exist. I felt numb and it was as though the earth beneath me had disappeared. This was my turning point, my moment to choose. I stood there thinking, I have a choice, what will it be? (Looking back, this was one of those questions I was asking my "wise self", as I wasn't really conscious there was two of me at the time.) The voice in my head had changed. It was no longer saying to me: Why is he being mean? Why can't he just understand what I'm going through? That voice came from the wounded ego. This new voice was my true self and I heard it say: We have to take charge now, forget about the whys, forget about the whining, we need to take a stand or this body is going down. I made a pact with myself: that from that day on I was going to be completely honest and vulnerable. I wanted to wake up. I wanted to be happy and I wanted to be true to myself: no matter what. I really believe this is the number one step to consciousness; waking up to the life you want and being healthy and happy. I became aware I was going to be fine and it was my mind that had convinced me otherwise and confused me. I had met me at my core: the wise, confident and secure me.

We aren't honest because we're afraid of the consequences of being honest. The reason we're afraid in the first place is a result of our conditioning and what happened to us, possibly in past lives, but certainly as kids growing up. From my experience it wasn't ever okay to say how you felt.

Everything seemed clear to me now, the struggle I had been in for so long was gone. I wasn't going upstream anymore. I felt the letting go of the stories of my mind. I had allowed myself to be turned around to have the river take me downstream, to where I didn't know, but it felt easy and light and good and I trusted in that.

Later that day I told my husband he had to make a choice: stop having expectations I couldn't meet, stop getting angry at me, and listen to what I needed - or I would have to go. He was angry as I spoke these words, but somehow his fear and anger didn't have an effect on me any longer. I had broken down the wall I had been hiding behind all these years: the fear to speak my truth and I wasn't afraid any longer. I really didn't have the energy to be afraid.

In the next couple of days he changed too. Sometimes I wonder whether he came into my life to act this way so I could realize my own courage and learn to stand up for myself, because he became gentler. It was as though his job was done and he could stand down. Perhaps we had an unspoken contract when we entered into this life together that this was exactly what his job was, to help me to become all of me. It was a strange feeling.

Perhaps we are pushed to such levels because that's what it takes for us to wake up. I hated that I was so afraid for so long. If it were easy, perhaps we wouldn't fully understand the awakenings we have. My hope is that one day we won't have to fight so hard to be ourselves. Believe it or not, there are some people who do say what they feel and they also accept the consequences of this.

Perhaps that's what we are truly afraid of, the responsibility of being ourselves.

I read a great quote by Chief Joseph on surrendering that encapsulated the Native American experience and described the point I got to in my own exhaustion. *"Our chiefs are dead; the little children are freezing to death. My people have no blankets, no food ... I want to have time to look for my children and see how many I can find ... Hear me, my chiefs. I am tired. My heart is sick and sad. From where the sun now stands, I will fight no more."*

This is how I truly felt in that moment. Those are powerful words and to this day and I get goose bumps every time I read them. They simplified for me that all I had to do was to speak my truth; I had overcomplicated my thoughts. It taught me to get out of my mind and speak what is clearly in front of me without the fear of being judged, to ask for what I need, to speak my truth, just to say it. I overanalyzed my every thought and why? I had tried to find a way where peace would and could prevail, which in some circumstances I now know, just can't happen, at least not the way I want it to. There is peace hiding in conflict and I needed to understand that. This was a big learning lesson for me because this had been my fear all my life: knowing that to speak my truth would cause the wounded ego in another to be evoked terrified me and I would do anything to not let that happen which included compromising myself. I saw no way out, I had to stick up for myself and say: "No more, I will fight no more, I am done."

When you are with another person and faced with a conflict that seems to be going in circles and isn't resolving itself, then one of you has to take a stand. If faced with an overpowering, "No" in the past, I would have allowed that to win just to keep the peace, because I doubted myself. Now I just say what I'm feeling and I believe I have a right to speak my own truth. So, if you and another are trying to make a decision and come to a conclusion, you have to choose. Is it big enough that you may have to stand alone and do it anyway or will you compromise? You have to take responsibility, perhaps solely. There may be fear on both sides and this needs to be discussed. Belief creates the fear, so find out what the belief is, then decide if it's real. What you believe is keeping you stuck. Usually your wounded ego has been woken up and is in protection mode, thinking it's being helpful. Therefore, if what you believe is causing the conflict, what if it's not true? Can you change what you believe to change the outcome? What would you be giving up? Think about how your truth affects others. Well, from my experience, that's the vulnerability of becoming your authentic self. Are you prepared to be vulnerable and expose all of your thoughts?

It's about taking responsibility for yourself and how it affects others. It doesn't mean don't do or say it, it just means speak it, discuss it, not as a final destination, but as a detective trying to solve a crime. There isn't a right or wrong; there is just your truth and the other person's truth. The trick is to be able to come to a place in which you both feel you have been able to express your own truths and then be able to detach enough to allow each other's own final decisions. It's big, but not impossible. Usually one person is left happy and the other is left annoyed that he or she didn't win. The need to win always involves the ego. So, if you're left like this don't stop. Keep talking until you can find a place within you that uncovers the real reason you're still annoyed. Break it down to its smallest common denominator. Get to the bottom of what's bugging you and then express it. Don't be afraid to be vulnerable.

The reasons I felt sad came from the conflict between what I truly believed and what I was witnessing and dealing with in my life. It was the conflict that hurt me so much. The fact it went on and I couldn't communicate with my husband. I wanted it stopped; it wasn't okay with me anymore. As you're reading this, it may appear that there was a lot of conflict in my family, but that isn't true. We weren't any different than most families. The fact was I didn't have any tolerance for it. I will be the first to admit I'm not an easy person to be around. I have unusually high expectations of the ability to achieve a peaceful existence. I remember being told by a psychic I am altruistic, meaning I believe that by giving we are receiving at the same time. Therefore, it wasn't ever hard for me to give myself. I didn't see it as putting myself last, it was more about if I could give, I would, and most of the time I did. It isn't within my world to be hurtful or unkind; I really do believe we can coexist peacefully and respectfully. Oh, I know I'm not perfect and I don't try to be. I couldn't tolerate conflict, so I'd do anything to avoid it. I know for some this may seem impossible, but not for me. I also know it's a tall order and my poor husband has had to live with this zero tolerance of conflict our whole marriage. What really frightened me was the knowing the wounded ego exists in all of us and I was afraid of waking it up in others.

Later that week, Trevor and I went to see our naturopathic doctor. Trevor listened in and watched as the technician explained about my live blood cells floating around on the computer screen. They were thick, sticky, low in oxygen, and struggling to break free from one another. Trevor listened to the technician tell me once again that my adrenals were toast. It was then I suddenly had an epiphany. I realized I had created this, all of it. My poor body was trying to take care of me, but my thoughts and beliefs were causing it such grief. In my conflict within myself, I was making my body work too hard, I was asking too much of it. Tears slowly ran down my cheeks as this realization sunk in. I tried to hide them, but now I finally understood I had the control all along. I could change this and help my body to heal.

In his book *The Biology of Belief,* Bruce Lipton talks a lot about this fact. He says: "The longer you stay in protection, the more you consume your energy reserves. The proportion of cells in a protection response depends on the severity of the perceived threats, note perceived threats! To fully thrive we must not only eliminate the stressors but also actively seek joyful, loving, fulfilling lives that stimulate growth processes." He goes onto say: "Almost every major illness that people acquire has been linked to chronic stress." I would have to agree. When you realize what being in conflict with yourself is doing to the homeostasis of your body, you will relook at the load you are currently carrying and ask yourself why?

Lipton says: "Positive thoughts have a profound effect on behaviour and genes but only when they are in harmony with subconscious programming. And negative thoughts have an equally powerful effect. When we recognize how these positive and negative beliefs control our biology, we can use this knowledge to create lives filled with health and happiness. Put boldly, **fear shuts down growth**. It also makes us act stupid. It is not our genes but our beliefs that control our lives."

During our appointment with the naturopath, the technician said I had more red cells than normal because my body needed to get more oxygen and my adrenals were very stressed. I explained to him, with my husband still sitting in the room, that my son's divorce had taken its final toll on me. Later that afternoon we went into see the doctor and again I explained I had nothing left in me. I felt like sleeping all the time, I couldn't think straight, I had no desire for sex; it didn't come from my brain, it came from my body having nothing left to give.

Once again Bruce Lipton explains what happens to the adrenals. He says: "In response to perceptions of stress registered in the brain, the hypothalamus secretes a corticotrophin-releasing factor (CRF), which travels to the pituitary gland. CRF activates special pituitary hormone-secreting cells causing them to release adrenocorticotropic hormones (ACTH) into the blood. The ACTH then makes its way to the adrenal glands, where it serves as the signal to turn on the secretion of the 'fight-flight' adrenal hormones. These stress hormones coordinate the function of the body's organs providing us with great physiologic power to fend off or flee danger. Once the adrenal alarm is sounded, the stress hormones released into the blood constrict the blood vessels of the digestive tract, forcing the energy-providing blood to preferentially nourish the tissues of the arms and legs that enable us to get out of harm's way. Before the blood was sent to the extremities, it was concentrated in the visceral organs. Redistributing the viscera's blood to the limbs in the fight or flight response results in an inhibition of growth related functions; without the blood's nourishment the visceral organs cannot function properly. The visceral organs stop doing their life sustaining work of digestion, absorption, excretion, and other functions that provide for the growth of the cells and the production of the body's energy reserves. Hence the stress response inhibits growth process and further compromises the body's survival by interfering with the generation of vital energy reserves."

Lipton goes on to talk about the immune system and how the adrenals play a role in that, too. He asks the question: "Why would the adrenal system shut down the immune system? Imagine you are in your tent in Africa suffering from a bacterial infection and experiencing a bad case of diarrhea. You hear a lion outside your tent. The brain has to make a decision about which is the greatest threat. It will do your body no good to conquer the bacteria if you let a lion maul you. So your body halts the fight against the infection in favour of mobilizing energy for the fight to survive your close encounter with a lion. Therefore a secondary consequence of engaging the HPA axis is that it interferes with our ability to fight disease. It also interferes with our ability to think clearly. The HPA system is a brilliant mechanism for handling acute stresses. However, this protection system was not designed to be continuously activated. In today's world, most of the stresses we are experiencing are not in the form of acute, concrete 'threats' that we can easily identify, respond to, and move on. We are constantly besieged by multitudes of irresolvable worries about our personal lives, our jobs, and our war-torn global community. Such worries do not threaten our immediate survival, but they nevertheless can activate the HPA axis, resulting in chronically elevated stress hormones."

All this information may be a bit technical to follow, but the point I'm trying to make is that if you think stress doesn't play the major role in your health and happiness, then you are kidding yourself. Ask yourself: What stresses you out? Right now, what is sitting heavily on your mind? I suggest that you work towards emptying your bucket of all the things you're afraid to do and say; make a list of what they are. When you do this with understanding and compassion, this will go a long way to conquering the current stresses in your life and improve your health. We lay such a heavy blanket on top of all our fears. Take off the blanket and let the worries out into the open. You will see how much better, happier, and healthier you will feel. Know that almost all of these worries don't need to stay inside your body.

In the book *Adrenal Fatigue*, Dr. Wilson's says: "People will tell you that happiness is a choice so choose to be happy but when you have adrenal fatigue that is not an option; your body doesn't have the required brain chemistry to get you to feel happy."

I found reading this was extremely helpful because my husband is a positive guy and he would always say: "Just choose to be happy." Yet that would make me feel even worse. Now, having the discussion with both my naturopath and husband present was helpful because Trevor was now able to hear me and understand why it was so hard for me to find my happiness within me.

After my session, it was Trevor's turn. The doctor told him that he, too, had fatigued adrenals. He also had high blood pressure, high cholesterol, anxiety, and his heartbeat was too fast. He agreed he had been anxious lately because he didn't know what to do with me or how to help me. Men like to "fix" things, but what was wrong with me was something only I could fix. A lot of partners get anxious because they don't know how to help their spouses. What they need to do is respect what their partners are asking of them and not question it to the point at which it turns out to be about them. It frustrated me so much when my husband did this. It didn't matter what I asked of him, it always turned to being about his needs. I made him anxious and he needed to find out how to relieve that feeling within him and the only way he believed this could happen was to fix me, ugh, sound familiar?

Our partners don't understand that when we have let ourselves get that low, we don't care about anything or anyone. As a result they get mad at us because they're scared, but really our body's mechanics simply don't have what we need to care. It's not a choice at that point and I believe this is our body's only way of getting us to realize we have to be selfish to take care of ourselves. Self-care is the prescription. Of course, it's not selfish, but that's how society looks at it. We need to change that. The core problem here is that we don't respect each other or ourselves enough. Those of us in relationships still believe we need something from each other. We need to back off and realize we don't need anything. A real relationship is built on respect and allowing each person to be all he or she can and wants to be.

There is a story about a family whose neighbour was a monk. The family's 16-year-old daughter got pregnant and the daughter accused the monk of being the father, so when the baby was born, they took the baby around to the monk's house and said: "Here, he's your responsibility, you bring him up." The monk took the baby without protest and brought the child up as his own. Years later, the daughter admitted to the parents the child wasn't the monk's and took the child back. The monk said nothing.

The point is: the monk took in this child and brought him up without defending himself. We can learn from the monk; for example, in relationships we think we need to defend our decisions and ourselves and we don't. In my recovery, I needed to take care of myself, but I was met with anger and frustration and this took me further away from recovering. I knew what I needed to get better, but I couldn't get those around me to understand. So I had to fight that off too, or so I thought. In fact, I learned I didn't need to defend myself. I just needed to do what I could to take care of myself. That's my journey and if others don't understand this, then it's up to them to try to get to the bottom of whatever it is they are feeling. That's their journey. As I see it, no one can take care of you but you, so stop waiting for someone else to help you. You must make your own stand. I have eight sisters and all of us, in our own ways, have had to learn this lesson; why? Because we weren't taught to stand up for ourselves; however, what hurts the most is when you see you have passed this conditioning onto your own children.

Too often the person in the family who gets sick is the one who doesn't know how or what to do and then those around them don't know either, then you have a bunch of scared and freaked out people. Usually communication shuts down, because if it opens up, it's usually expressed with anger or fear, which isn't helpful. It seems to me we're all coming from the wounded ego. We need to learn to step outside ourselves and treat one another like good friends, no matter whether we're interacting with family, partners, kids, or others. Basically, we have lost respect and this situation is making everyone scared and acting out. I watched a "Ted Talk" once with a doctor saying how it's not our bodies that make us sick, it's our relationships, and I believe this to be so true. It's the relationship we have with ourselves, or others, but more often it's both. If we heal those, we can heal our bodies.

I believe we should be practicing respectful communication; for example, I get to say what I need and you get to say what you need. We have to understand we don't get to be in control of anyone else but ourselves, no matter what. Relationships are a choice and ultimately we all make a choice to stay in them or not, but we don't have the right to blame, dictate, or be angry just because we don't get what we want or think we need. We want to believe our hearts are broken so that's supposed to justify our behaviour, but this isn't true. It's not that our hearts are broken; it's that our egos are wounded.

The heart isn't capable of anger and meanness; only love. It's the wounded ego that gets hurt, angry and wants to lay blame. When we truly come to understand what it means to "love," then we will have respectful relationships. Remember the saying: "If you love them, let them go." That is love. That quote means you haven't control over another. When love becomes your guide, you lead with love for yourself, then others will follow and relationships can be healed. It's the transformation that happens naturally when there is unconditional love, first for you and then for others.

An example of this happened a year later … as I was leaving for our big trip around the world on our motorcycle in 2009; my daughter told me she was angry with me for going. I said I understood, but I felt it was time for me to go on this trip for both her and me. She cried and let out her emotions, the next day when she said goodbye she told me she wasn't sad or mad anymore and was okay with me going. She had been heard and that's all she needed. When her dad heard about this, he said she was being selfish. This is exactly why we humans have so many problems. We are brought up to think it's not okay to tell the truth about how we feel. We keep it suppressed and then we are screwed up down the road. My husband's conditioning caused him to reply this way. Perhaps if he had been able to truly express himself when he was young, when his dad was abusive to him, he would have been completely okay with our daughter's response. We have to get rid of this belief system that dictates it's only okay to tell the truth when it's not going to hurt someone. How are we to know if our words are going to hurt someone else by what we believe to be true, which may not necessarily be "the" truth? The truth is only our truth. How are we to ever figure anything out if we don't tell our truth? How are we to evolve?

In today's world, why do you think there are so many therapists? As I see it, in their presence we humans finally feel brave enough to tell the truth. Why didn't we just do that as kids? And why wasn't it okay with our parents back then? Imagine how different things would be today. I highly doubt we would need so many therapists if that had been the case. Our daughter was expressing how she felt to me in a safe environment. I wasn't defensive about the need to go on my trip; I didn't get angry with her. I simply said I understood how she felt and I acknowledged her pain. The bottom line is we all want acknowledgement of how we are feeling. If you look into any relationship problems, it's not about each person agreeing with the other; it's about being heard and considered. Human beings don't like the feeling that others have control over them, it's definitely what wakes up the wounded ego within them.

Another interesting conversation I heard when I started out on our trip was when I was sitting outside on the restaurant's patio and I overheard a couple of older ladies discussing what God would have to say about one of them wanting to visit her husband's family without him. The woman in question had asked her husband to go with her, but he didn't want to, so she was asking her friend if she should go alone. I thought to myself: What has this world come to? Why are we so afraid all the time to do what we want? Where did we get taught that if we don't do what our partner wants us to do, we're bad and will get into trouble? I believe it's our conditioning. A friend calls this "Christian conditioning". It's not that God thinks like this, he doesn't. We were just taught to behave this way. I know I was and I taught my kids this belief as well. How I wish I hadn't. Now I'm teaching them to stick up for themselves. I thought I was being a nice person back then: When people treat you wrongly just walk away, the whole turn-the-other-cheek thing. What message are we sending to our kids? That they don't matter, as long as everyone else is okay, it's all good. I think not. What this actually means is, don't bite the hook, and don't pick a fight. Certainly it didn't mean walk away and feel as though you don't matter. I believe it's important to stay around and get to the bottom of what's going on, ask questions, come from your own power, not from your wounded ego. If my parents had taught me that, I would have been so much better off and so would my kids. How misunderstood those Biblical teachings can be.

Shortly after, my daughter encountered another situation about having to be honest. One of her good friends phoned and asked her to do a favour. My daughter hesitated and said if she couldn't find anyone else to help her out, then she would do it. The friend replied: "Just tell me the truth, if you don't want to then that's fine, I'll find someone else." So my daughter replied: "Okay, then I'm tired and I don't really want to." There was a long silence on the phone, my daughter called her name to make sure she was still on the line and her friend was mad. From that experience she learned the message it's not okay to be honest or else people will be mad at us. She could have followed up with: "Are you mad at me?" And if her friend had said yes, then she could have added: "Well you told me to tell you the truth and I did, so you can't be mad at me."

Who said you had to sacrifice yourself for the love of another? If you choose to continue to do this, you will eventually become resentful and you will be in conflict with your true self and this will make you sick. Furthermore, when you harbor resentment, you can't love someone from the same place, believe me, this is what I used to do. I didn't like who I had become. I was short with Trevor at times, unconsciously unaware of my own behaviour because I resented him believing he could control who I was. He didn't have a clue about any of this, but that didn't matter because what I believed created my world and made me unhappy. I just kept thinking aren't I enough? Aren't I a good enough person in my own right? Why do I have to conform to be loved? Why do I have to say yes when I want to say no?

At my very lowest point, I saw the truth of what had happened to me. Our son's divorce had taken me beyond myself, to a place I didn't recognize. It had taken me to the smallest common denominator of who I am at my core, something I never managed to be able to reach consciously before. It was as though I found myself as a seed again, before I became conditioned. I found out who I really am and I could now see my truth.

Dr. Wilson's book, *Adrenal Fatigue*, came into my life just when I needed it most. I hadn't been taught how to take care of myself, given that this was "selfish", according to my childhood beliefs. The book is well written and along with great tools to help you step by step, it also has some very humorous diagrams that take the seriousness out of illness.

For me depression was a gift. Don't get me wrong, at the time it didn't feel like a gift. However, looking back I realize it was given to me to step into my own courage. It sent me on a mission to find out why this was happening, to reflect on my life, and discover what action I needed to take. I watched my own mother go through depression when I was fourteen years old. I was just a child trying to get through high school. I would come home to find her sleeping in the living room every day, too depressed to care about me, herself or anyone else for that matter. I knew she was depressed and I knew why: My father had moved us back to England and my mother hated it. She never wanted to make the move, she said yes when she wanted to say no. She wasn't in control of her own life and felt helpless to ever change it. She agreed to something she didn't want, she went against herself. She internalized all this grief; she didn't express herself and thereby setting the adrenal depletion in motion, which led to her full on depression.

Some good questions to ask yourself are: In my life what don't I feel in control of? Do I speak my truth, if not why?

In his book, *Biology of Belief*, Dr. Lipton says, "When your conscious mind has a belief that is in conflict with a formerly learned truth stored in the subconscious mind, the intellectual conflict expresses itself as a weakening of the body's muscles." This makes it pretty clear our minds are controlling what's happening to our bodies ... it's about what we believe and how we think, which is responsible for our health.

We are all so stressed out trying to get by doing the right thing, being the right thing, saying the right thing, we end up burnt out and don't know why until it's too late and finally our physical body starts to show signs we have pushed ourselves too far and we get sick. Our expectations of ourselves are over the top and not sustainable. We live in a society of greed in which we never feel as though we're enough. What we have will never be enough, so we spend our whole lives trying to be something we're not, trying to get somewhere we can't. We set ourselves up to fail, so we fall into depression. Either we bring this on ourselves, or we live with people who make us feel this way (at least we believe they do). Either way, both lead to disaster, yet the responsibility still lies with us. We have abandoned ourselves. We have lost touch with ourselves, we have conformed to others' ways, or our own misguided beliefs about how we should be and we adapt to what our society, family, friends want us to be. What happened to what we want? Who we really are? And why can't we be our authentic selves? Aren't we enough?

There is a quiet place beyond the mind where we can connect to this knowing that we are and have always been just fine, where we know how to take care of ourselves. This goes hand-in-hand with understanding the wounded ego doesn't have to be in control of our lives. This is the duality, the two parts within one body, the all-knowing self and the wounded self: consciousness is to know both. The wounded ego loves to complain, whine, react, and it loves company. When you remove yourself from the people and things that don't serve you anymore and are in fact taking from you, you begin to realize you have recognized the ego has been in control of your life, its needed the people in your life to keep you from seeing your truth.

You may ask: Why do we listen to it when life isn't working for us? Even though the ego's decisions make us miserable, we listen because we don't know it's there and haven't yet realized it's not our true self we're hearing. It's the voice of our ego. The ego is like an overprotective parent who thinks it actually knows what's better for you than you do for yourself. It's always afraid for you and worries you will get yourself into trouble and it can't bear the pain. "It" being the key word. It can also be compared to a child, the child in all of us who is afraid. Just like children and parents, it's the "not being in control" that the ego is afraid of, that's why its reactions come in the form of aggression or submission. (Ego represents the fear that is within each one of us, what that fear is and where it came from is different for everyone.)

Deepak Chopra said in *The Book of Secrets,* "Change is frightening, but more than that it is threatening to the ego."

I was stuck in the belief that I couldn't be me; I was waiting for permission. Every time I tried to be me, my ego would go into fear and I would retreat believing that it wasn't safe. This belief is of my ego, it was a perceived threat, not a real threat to my safety, yet it kept me controlled and stuck. It wasn't until I stepped out of this belief and realized that I wasn't in any real danger and changed my belief that I was then able to create a new belief. I was allowed to be me and I would still be safe and loved.

This has been called "Circular Thinking", which is sometimes mixed up with obsession. For example, a phrase comes to mind, "You can't solve the problems with the same mind you created them with." That's why people who are stuck in circular thinking can't find their way out, it's very hard to question your beliefs and realize that you have the power to change them. You have probably met the character who always feels unloved. It is frustrating to express love for them when they deny how you feel about them because they don't feel loved. Inside, their ego is having a battle. "I want love and this person is saying he loves me, but I can't feel it, which must mean they do not love me."

The only way they can fix that is to get love. The belief that they have to get love prevents them from being able to feel love: it's not that they aren't loved. They look for love in the wrong places, outside of themselves, believing they have to "take" love. So they are creating their own reality, because to take love will never allow them to feel loved. We all know people like this, those who never felt successful enough (maybe they were told as a child they will never succeed), they never felt wanted (even in the womb the child will know if they are wanted or not), and whatever they do to try and change from the outside, will only reinforce their original belief.

We create "Circular Thinking" as a tool to gain control. It's a belief that keeps us feeling in power, so we keep going there and repeating it and then we get stuck in a loop. Investigate as I did why you are afraid of losing control? What would happen if you stepped out of the circle or believed in something different? Take a deep breath and allow yourself to visualize letting go of control. What emotions are coming up for you? If it's fear, fear of what? Keep going into the fear and digging a deep path to its core. When you get to the bottom, you will know and in this knowing light is brought to the darkness, which will free you from this circular thinking. This is consciousness; it's pure healing. The reason it's so hard to do on your own is the feeling of fear that arises within you is so strong and frightening you will want to retreat, but trust me, it's just your ego in fear, it's trapped energy needing and wanting to escape and to leave you in peace. If you have someone you trust to be there and hold your hand, to encourage you, this will make it easier.

A depressed person thinks of countless things, but acts on none of them. So getting back to the moment when it dawns on you that, "nobody can take care of you but you," is the moment you have recognized the ego by letting go of all that it's taking from you is the very thing the ego has been keeping you from discovering. People who take time out for themselves are seeking the calm of solitude, where external demands are fewer. In its natural state, the mind stops reacting once external stimulation goes away. This is why nature is key: it gives and never takes. I suggest that you remove yourself from all that takes you from you; you will discover that you actually start to relax. Once you become aware of how different you feel, you can start to find out why those things affected you, and how your wounded ego kept you in that circular trap. Even if you don't know why situations feel like they are taking something from you, it doesn't matter, step away from them for a while to break the cycle. Finding a place of solitude is like escaping the waves in the river's shallows to find a depth where the current slows down. Your thoughts keep moving, but they aren't so insistent that they push you forward. This has become my meditation spot and how I learned to detach myself from my wounded ego so I could watch it. I visualize myself sitting on a river bed (my true self) as the turbulence (my wounded ego) on the surface continues to rush over me, yet I am calm and relaxed because I have stepped out of the exterior noise (my mind) and moved into the interior of my body (my listening centre where all answers lie). If we're quiet and listen really well, our bodies speak to us and we can finally hear.

In short, we have lost the ability to listen to our own bodies and the wisdom within them that can only be heard when our minds are quiet. When my father was dying, I remember giving him a small picture with the words: "When the heart speaks, the mind is quiet," this was a constant reminder to me to quiet my mind and let go and breathe.

I want to finish this chapter with more quotes from Dr. Wilson's book. For me it was about being given permission to take care of myself. Isn't it strange that we need that? He says: "Tired, worn-out, just can't regain your normal energy no matter what you do or how many doctors you visit? You're about to read an important and badly needed book. Despite an absolute flood of 'health books' in the last decade, there have been none that describes the not uncommon, mostly overlooked problem of adrenal gland function in such a thorough but understandable way. The answers you're looking for may well lie here in this book."

"Adrenal Fatigue (technically called 'hypoadrenia' and 'hypoadrenalism') has been one of our most prevalent yet rarely diagnosed conditions for the last fifty years. Despite being described in medical texts in the 1800s and despite the development of the first really effective treatment in the 1930s, most conventional physicians are unaware that the problem exists."

"There are lifestyle changes to be made, diets to alter forever (sometimes in a major way), vitamins and herbs to swallow, tests to take and understand and much patience required. Even attitude and relationships sometimes need to be adjusted."

From reading his book I discovered it's a commitment to yourself to take your health into your own hands and free yourself from being a victim of illness into empowering yourself to be your authentic self. I followed the book and its recommendations; from what I ate to what time I woke in the morning and how I kept myself away from people and situations that only "took" from me. I spent time with people and situations that only "gave" to me. I became "selfish," self-caring for a year and looked after myself, even while still being in my own family; I just told them that's what I needed. I finally spoke up for myself and it didn't matter what the response was, I knew I had to. I still worked at my job and did the best I could in all areas of my life.

Our Western ways have done little to help us understand the balance of life and what it means to take care of ourselves. In the East, people take time out for themselves in many ways. They give themselves permission. We Westerners just keep pushing and running to where and what we don't even know ourselves. We're caught up in the rat race of life. I hope you learn more of the ways of the East and step into your own recovery. Behind vulnerability and the fear to speak your truth is joy. There isn't a drug to cure adrenal fatigue, the only cure is you: Step into your courage and your own powerful ability to heal and become your authentic self and go forward to live the life you came here for.

NOTE:

Chapter Nine of Dr. Wilson's book, *How Did I Get This Way*, is brilliant. In it, you fill out a health history timeline. It asks for dates and incidents of surgeries, hospital visits, sicknesses, dental work, emotional events, such as job changes, moving, death of loved ones, separation, divorce, financial difficulties, shocks, traumas, and finally about prescription drugs you've ever taken. I found this so interesting and informative, because once I began identifying my life events; I could start to see why I had this problem.

Chapter Ten: *Tests for Adrenal Fatigue You Can do at Home* is another great chapter. I always had low blood pressure and a low pulse; I believed this to be genetic. It wasn't, it's a sign of adrenal fatigue. I was also hypoglycemic, another sign.

Did you know the energetic explanation for hypoglycemia or diabetes is "a loss of the sweetness of life?" I like that. It's sad, but it really does feel that way when you're in it. For me, it was sad that I knew I created my health challenges by believing I wasn't allowed to be all of me. I find it fascinating that what we believe has so much power over us and creates our reality.

CHAPTER NINE

Shining Light into the Darkness

⌒

Song: "Realize" by Colbie Caillat

I first came across Eliza Mada Dalian in April, 2009 when I was searching for a name for my book. I typed "Evolving into Consciousness" into Google's search parameters and Mada's book *In Search of the Miraculous: Healing into Consciousness* came up. As I read the introduction and reviews I thought, Hmm I don't need to write my book, she has already written what I wanted to say. I Googled her further and found her website. It turned out she lived in Vancouver and offered private sessions, so I booked an appointment. At that time I was more curious to experience what she did; not so much to fix a problem.

A few weeks later, as she opened the door to her condo I was surprised to see standing in front of me someone who looked a lot like me. It caught me off guard. She was similar in height and build, but it was her hair that most resembled mine, blonde and very curly. She was all smiles and there appeared to be two of her because the mirrored doors in the entranceway reflected her in two of them. I wasn't sure which one to talk to, which felt very odd but really funny at the same time. We both laughed and it broke my nervousness.

As she showed me to where to sit in the living room, I noticed her choice in books was also similar to mine. Buddha statues sat on the shelves and there was a sense of quiet and calmness in her home. I started to feel more comfortable. She sat in a big comfy chair and seated me across from her. I looked directly into her eyes and they radiated back a pure inner wisdom, they sparkled. She seemed happy and childlike, as though she knew a secret and couldn't wait to tell me. I was excited but anxious at the same time. I started chatting. Anyone who knows me knows I talk a lot and quite fast. I was telling her I wanted to make some changes in my career and wasn't sure how to go about it. After about ten minutes she stopped me and said she could already see from reading my energy that there was work to do and because I had only booked a short session, we needed to get started. She had me uncross my legs, plant my feet firmly on the ground, and place my hands on my knees. Then she had me breathe deeply into my belly and exhale. On the second breath, she started to read what was in my body. She said breathe again into your belly and look inside yourself. That felt odd, but I did the best I could.

On the next breath she said: "I can see you are a very courageous soul, but based on how you grew up, your self-confidence isn't there. You have courage, but not having the confidence is undermining your courage." She continued: "This programming has been set inside of you from a young age, from likely something you heard, or perhaps someone said something to you. We need to change your programming." Then she told me to breathe again and asked what number sister I was. "Number eight," I replied. She said: "There is a belief in you that 'I'm not smart enough,' which has created the lack of self-confidence."

She had me breathe in again and then exhale out of my solar plexus. "Secondly, you have a pattern of stubbornness, the attitude that, 'I'm not going to move.' We need to see why it is there and what it is rooted in." Mada then informed me that coming from a large family, this stubbornness has helped me to hold onto my individuality: "It's been a positive force and helpful while growing up. Your intelligence knew at an early age that you are an individual and have your own voice. Your energy says, 'I'm going to stay firm, I'm not going to let other people dictate to me.' In spite of this, however, the belief, 'I'm not smart enough' is compromising your inner clarity and opportunity to see that you are no longer a child and don't need to stubbornly fight for your independence." She pointed out not wanting to be told what to do had both helped and hindered me in life and the belief I need to fight to be me was creating inner tension and not allowing me to relax.

Mada asserted: "You already know these beliefs are not serving you anymore and it's time to let go, and that's why you're here." Then she had me breathe again, express the thought forms she was reading in my energy out loud and exhale. Tears started rolling down my face as I blurted out concerns about my mother: her fears, her being Catholic, her resistance, and her faith. Though I couldn't really make sense of what was happening and what I was supposed to see, I recognized that I didn't receive nourishment from my mother, emotionally, and concluded that growing up life was hard. I suddenly felt sad for myself. I also believed I was alone and had to struggle.

It was such a surprise Mada was able to read my beliefs through watching me breathe. What she was saying felt like a light penetrating into my inner darkness. It brought up resistance, surprise, and emotions all at the same time. I knew what she was pointing to was real and true.

Up to this point she was identifying what was in my energy so she could see the root cause of where my energy was blocked. The next step was to help me release the beliefs that weren't serving me any longer. She instructed me to breathe into my belly and out of my left shoulder. I have lived with chronic pain in that shoulder for most of my life, well; as far back as I can remember. I thought it was due to working on a computer. As I breathed out through my shoulder, she said there had been a betrayal in this life or another one and I was still holding onto the feelings.

"You are still holding on to the hurt and can't let go, can you recall anything?" she asked. I didn't know what she was referring to for a moment. I tried to figure out what the word betrayed was associated with, but couldn't. All I could say was one of my sister's names came to mind. Mada and I worked on this for quite a while through her technique (the Dalian Method) of breathing and out loud expression, and as it turned out, I did feel betrayed.

I'd trusted my sister my whole life. I knew who she was, but then discovered she wasn't always who she seemed to be and I felt betrayed. I was still carrying the hurt, even though my mind had managed to come to terms with it, my body was still holding on. This was a big realization and new understanding.

On the right side of my energy we worked with the belief, "I'm afraid" and on my left, "I don't deserve," both were keeping me stuck. Mada said these beliefs (imprinted in my energy) were dictating how my life was unfolding and they needed to be transformed into consciousness. Other repressed thought forms we worked with were: I'm not good enough and I don't deserve to receive anything; I'm not smart enough and everybody thinks I'm not smart enough; nobody cares about me and I'm all alone; I'm afraid and I don't know what to do; and I hate myself for not knowing what to do.

I'm not going to go into all of the conversation, but what happened as a result of releasing these repressed thought forms was my voice grew louder and stronger. I could feel a shift taking place within me. I felt more confident and fearless. I realized I'm not stupid and I didn't need to fight to stand up for myself. I felt more love towards myself and confident in my own abilities. I felt as though a ball of energy moved out of my hands and my feet. My body vibrated with freedom and joy physically. I felt completely relaxed and calm, with a sense of having let go of the things that weren't serving me any longer.

Within an hour, Mada helped to remove these old programs from my body and had transformed my fears and perception of reality. She then gave me three things to do for homework: one was to take flowers to my mother's grave and say thank you; secondly, was to explain to Trevor what I had discovered about myself with regards to being attached to him and his behaviours; thirdly, was to be able to be in my sisters' presence with compassion and without being attached to their fears.

Before the session, I felt as though I had been carrying so much around in my body and it felt heavy and waited down. My mind was overactive with thoughts and issues constantly seeking answers. Now, I didn't seem to be over processing. I felt calmer and lighter and my mind wasn't always consumed by how everything I did would affect others, now it felt quiet. Mada helped me to see that life after life we accumulate many layers of beliefs and conditionings, emotional hurt, fear, doubt, heartbreak, betrayal, or abuse. Life becomes a struggle. The weight of our unresolved issues forces us to suffer through depression, unhappiness, and pain. When we have suffered and learned enough, life forces us in its own way to peel away the layers we're holding onto. I discovered we don't need to waste years of our precious life struggling. We can speed up the healing process and enjoy living our life fully: if we know how to access and remove the unconscious imprints from our body.

I like this way of thinking. It makes logical sense to me and God knows I'm not a patient woman. I like the quick approach. I don't even mind suffering if it's just going to be for a short time. I never did believe or like it when people would say there is never a quick fix. As I see it, everything depends on how sick you are of being a victim to your own thoughts and beliefs and how stubbornly your ego wishes to hold onto that which no longer serves you.

I took the ferry back home and slept the whole way. I was feeling drained and empty, but in a good way. I felt peaceful, relieved, and more centred. When I got back home, I told Trevor all about Mada and what had happened. He was quite intrigued; it made sense to him too. So I asked Mada if she would give a workshop on Salt Spring Island and also have time to do some private sessions. She agreed. While I hadn't done anything like this before, I was so excited by her work and I wanted others to be able to experience it as well.

We held the workshop in our home as we had a huge workout room that could accommodate a large group. Twenty-one people showed up for the event, nineteen women and two men, one of which was my husband. What a brave man, ignorance is bliss isn't it? He didn't have a clue what he was in for! Or so I thought. Mada and her assistant, Kindi, arrived at our home the day before the workshop. It was very interesting having an enlightened being stay with us for a few days. No one can pull the wool over Mada's eyes. She sees things the way they are, she has no judgment about anything because she knows we're on our journey and that whatever is happening in our lives is required.

Trevor decided he would have a session with Mada the first evening she arrived. I was really nervous because I thought he might pull out at the last minute, but he didn't. Kindi and I went into town to have a coffee; I thought it best if we weren't there. When we returned, they had finished the session. The house felt very surreal - quiet, yet hard to explain. I was anxious, as I didn't know what to expect. Trevor just kept smiling at me, but I couldn't read him. For years I'd been able to feel his energy; now it seemed as though quiet surrounded him. What had happened in their session? I didn't pressure him to tell me, but I was dying to know. We went for a walk and still he said very little but kept smiling at me. What did that mean? Of course I wanted to know, but I didn't want to pry until he was ready to tell me. That evening, we all sat down to dinner together and discussed life and enlightenment and what that all meant. Trevor never liked the whole idea of becoming enlightened because he believed that meant being alone and he definitely didn't want that. When he asked Mada about this, she said it wasn't true but: "it's a common belief in our society." Mada doesn't say more than she needs to; she is clear and confident in a compelling sort of way. The evening reminded me of the many times my dad and I would talk about such things and it made me miss him and realize how much he would have loved to have been there with us.

As I climbed into bed that night, I still was confused and none the wiser about what Trevor and Mada had talked about. I slinked over to Trevor's side of the bed and looked down at him and said: "You feel different, and it feels like I'm in bed with a different man." It really did. He looked up at me and said: "Yeah, I'm sorry I've been pressuring you into sex all these years by manipulating and controlling you. I won't do that anymore." Well, you can imagine what thoughts were running through my head. It was hard for me to even comprehend he was saying; what I was hearing; he said it so gently and calmly. My heart softened and tears flowed down my cheeks: I wasn't used to hearing such understanding words from him. You can't even imagine what an impact this moment had on my heart and me! I felt so safe. How could one session with Mada bring about such change? We held each other and drifted off to sleep.

In the morning, before the workshop, Mada, Kindi, and I took a walk outside our house that is surrounded with farmland - there's nothing but horses in the fields, chickens running free, and sheep grazing along the pastures. It felt as though we had known one another before, kindred spirits who had come together in this lifetime, perhaps to continue with something from a previous life. It was lovely, like finding your tribe.

Soon after it was time for the workshop to begin. Mada sat in front of us as we arranged the chairs in a semi-circle. I was thrilled. People had come from all over. Some were women I worked with; some were friends, and some I didn't even know. I thought how brave everyone was for coming and sharing their deep thoughts and pain. One woman, who I knew from work, had cancer. She was amazing when she spoke to the group. Mada asked her: "How has having cancer changed your life?" She replied: "I no longer have time to waste, the type of cancer I have is in my whole body, so I only spend my energy on things that really matter to me. I'm honest with people and I don't waste my time with things that aren't important anymore. It's made me more focused on what I want to do before I'm too sick to do it."

Mada told us when people get this sick and are facing death, they realize they have very little time left and become more of their authentic selves for their remaining time - yet we don't need to wait until we become sick to be ourselves. I ended up partnering with this woman during the day. It was sad to find out her daughter didn't speak to her. Her daughter's lifestyle wasn't suitable for her daughter so the older woman had taken guardianship of her granddaughter.

Mada sat for a moment, asked us three questions and had us write them down on a piece of paper: If you are aware of a physical discomfort in your body, what is it? Where is it? And, what emotion would you say is it attached to? She urged us not to over-think or judge our responses; just note what first came to mind.

I wrote about a pain in my back and the thought was, I'm stuck; second was my consistently itchy little toe on my left foot. The emotions associated with it were annoyance and frustration. The outcome was to bring clarity to why it was there and what I needed to shift for it to go. I also wrote about a pain in my neck and the emotion was I don't want to carry people anymore.

She then asked us: "What are you afraid of? I wrote: I'm afraid to speak my truth; I'm afraid to be me; for the fear of being rejected and upsetting people.

Following this Mada went around the room and had each of us breathe in and out individually while she did a reading on our energy field. Then, she confirmed what was stuck in our energy and had us write it down. When she came to me, she told me I was stuck and frustrated and I didn't know what to do.

Then she had us pair up and I suddenly became anxious because my husband was standing beside me. I knew he would pick me as his partner, but I didn't want him because I didn't think I would be able to speak honestly with him. After all, I had arranged this workshop and I wanted to get something out of it! I looked over at Mada and she smiled and nodded as if to say, *It will be okay.* Shit, how can it be? I thought. I know Trevor; he won't understand or like what I have to say, and all these people will know. Then, I thought, what the hell, if not now then when? With Mada sitting in the room and twenty other people to support me: if I can't speak my truth now, then when? So I went for it.

I looked at Trevor and it's as if he knew what I was thinking. He smiled and said: "It's okay, don't worry, I am not afraid of anything now." There it was again, that unfamiliar calmness in him I wasn't used to. I looked over at Mada again; she smiled and nodded, as though assuring me it would be fine. Then I thought, Crap, so he is my partner, I guess I'm not getting out of this.

She had us pick numbers and letters and I fell into the trap of picking B and two. Trevor got A and one. Then Mada said: "B goes first," and I realized that wasn't working in my favour, either. I had thought perhaps if Trevor went first, I would find out things about his session with her and feel much safer, but it wasn't meant to be. We stood directly across from each other and I had to say what I was afraid of. As I looked into his eyes, I told him: "I'm afraid to be me, I'm afraid to tell the truth, because you will get mad at me and won't like it. I'm afraid of being rejected and upsetting people and I don't want to be afraid anymore." Tears rolled down my cheeks as I repeated this several times. It felt like torture. The more I said it, the more the tears came. You may think this was easy but it wasn't; quite frankly, I'd rather have been delivering a baby, because at least I would have known the outcome likely would be positive. I still didn't know how my husband would react to what I told him. I could only know how he would have reacted a few days back and that's what scared me. To my glorious surprise, he sat there looking at me with tears in his eyes, saying *I understand!* Oh my God, I thought the angels had landed, who is this man before me? Trevor looked at me, his eyes still filled with tears; he kept smiling and saying: "I know, I know." What had she done to him? He seemed so different. He was so gentle, kind, and compassionate. It made me feel as though I was in uncharted waters and how far dare I go? Then Trevor had to say what he was afraid of. He told me: "At this time I'm not afraid of anything." He repeated: "I know, I know." I thought, great, this isn't going to work. Of course, he's afraid of something. I questioned that he wasn't telling the truth.

He explained that after the session with Mada the day before, he didn't have any fears any longer; he'd gotten rid of them, so he said again: "I'm not afraid of anything." She had told him he was afraid to be alone, and because of this he has been trying to control and manipulate me into doing what he needed. Well, can you imagine the tears now? Here was my husband standing in front of me admitting with ease and without any fear what I had felt he had been doing all these years. I had tried to be myself, which he hadn't allowed because of a fear he had. Yet, I was paying the price. How unfair was that? For the first time in many years I felt seen; I felt heard; I felt understood by him. Trevor finished with: "I am not afraid to be alone." I looked over at Mada and she smiled. I guess she knew he would be fine with me because of what they had gone through the day before.

Many other things happened that day. We did active meditations, danced, shared stories with one another, did the breathing exercises, and worked on releasing old patterns stuck in our energy. Then I worked on my toe and back issues. Mada had us breathe into those spots that were painful and through our own consciousness we went into the emotions that arose; thus, we could uncover why those pains were still there. Again, I felt a release of energy come out from my feet and my mouth and knew it had to do with the fear to speak my truth and the fact I didn't want to take care of anyone anymore. The room became very noisy at times; some of the group had to use pillows to shout into them to keep it from distracting the rest of us. It was amazing how brave people were. That day, I let go of two things: Fear to speak my truth and the need to carry anyone anymore. It didn't mean they stopped showing up in my life, but like a test I knew they weren't real, they were just thought patterns, old beliefs, they no longer carried any energy within me. From that day onwards, whenever those thoughts showed up I would push through and go into them, knowing I could, without fear, knowing they wouldn't control me any longer.

We broke for a potluck lunch and everyone filled their plates with nutritious food. It was a beautiful fall day - the sun was shining and the air was crisp and the birds chirped. As I sat down to eat my lunch, thoughts drifted through my mind about what had just happened and I felt completely overwhelmed. I suddenly felt nauseous. I needed some air. I put my plate down and darted for the front door. I couldn't make sense of what was happening to me. I was anxious and as I got to the top of our long driveway, I felt the need to heave and throw up. Tears streamed down my cheeks and now I was in a full emotional purge. I had spent twenty-eight years waiting for this day to come and never really knowing if it ever would. I realized I was letting go of all the emotional energy I had stored up inside me, the energy I put aside to take care of Trevor and carry his burdens since the day we met. Not that he asked me to, it's what my conditioning taught me to do. I thought it was my job. I realized my energy had been used up for this for so long and now I was grieving this, but happy it was over.

We didn't have to divide our energies into things that didn't serve either of us. For any of you who have grieved for anything or anyone, you'll know what I'm talking about. I was grieving for myself, for the years of suppression, of keeping myself small and safe. Trevor was cured of a deep fear that started when he was three years old. A fear that had taken hold of him long before I even knew him, yet it played such a huge role in our relationship and in our lives. Between my conditioning and the belief I needed to take care of people and help them figure out their stuff, my need for peace and my fear of conflict and his fear of abandonment, we had become entwined in this unspoken contract. After the release, I came back into the house feeling good and clear. I knew why I had thrown up; I knew I had purged and now I felt secure enough to finally let go. It was safe for me to come out.

After the workshop Trevor told me about his session with Mada, not in great detail but enough for me to read between the lines and understand. He said: "She was so compassionate with me," which seemed to make a huge impact on him. She was able to help him become conscious of a deep wound and release the abandonment issues that he had been holding onto all these years. When he was three years old he was taken to hospital for a hernia. It required an operation, but it was over the Christmas holidays and he had to stay there for two weeks. He cried, not understanding why his parents had to leave him; he thought he was going to be left there forever. He remembered standing in his cot looking out the window down into the parking lot watching his parents drive away thinking they were never coming back. That's when his fear of being alone and abandoned began and it formed part of his character. Now at fifty-two he finally released it. Every time during his life, anything made him feel afraid he would be alone, he would react like a three-year-old-child, terrified and irrational which was very confusing for the kids and me. We didn't know he was afraid to be alone; we couldn't make sense of it. Unfortunately, this block became part of our kids and our lives. His behaviour during the times he was afraid gave the kids and me the wrong messages and we didn't understand him.

As I mentioned earlier, we met when I was fifteen years old and at sixteen I broke up with him. This was the second time in his life he had been left alone and it increased his fear of abandonment. He felt alone and broken hearted again. He decided it was so painful he would shield and protect his heart so he'd never feel this way again. Months later, when we got back together, he held a part of himself back. He couldn't trust me with his heart and on some level I always knew this, but didn't really remember or realize how hurt he was from the breakup all those years ago. I certainly didn't know being left in the hospital at three years of age had affected him and neither did he. Mada got him to breathe into his body to uncover what lay behind the fear of abandonment. He was able to release the trapped energy that had caused him to act out this issue in his life. Unfortunately, it's rare for this kind of program to be discovered. As a result people's trapped energy seldom gets released and instead causes relationships to suffer. Imagine if all of us figured out what our triggers are and where they came from. Wouldn't that be helpful to our families and us? When we're triggered by something, it's helpful to take a deep breath and go inside to see if we can sense the belief; for example, the fear and where it came from.

The reason Trevor wanted sex so often was because it made him feel loved and for some men this can be the case. Women, on the other hand, need to feel loved to want to have sex, which is quite different. Even I didn't know this. I also realized that when I'm stressed; I don't want to have sex; however, when Trevor's stressed he needs to have sex. Men and women do operate differently, but even though this may be true, I believe having respect for each other is what's required.

A few months before the workshop I'd already had a shift. I realized that without having the kids around to protect I could come out of hiding (so to speak, not that I really ever knew I was keeping part of myself hidden). This shift brought out the realization that I needed to be one hundred percent me. I had returned to my true personality and to my surprise: I was able to love my husband on a deeper level after this shift happened. It seemed the more honest I became with my husband, and myself the happier that made me.

Before Mada, it was hard for Trevor to cope with the new outspoken and somewhat disagreeable me. Even though I was able to show him love, he still felt unsafe. I confused him, I think he thought because I was different I might leave - remember this was before the workshop. Of course I wasn't thinking of leaving, but he didn't know that. So he began behaving strangely, which I didn't understand. He was getting angry about things I would do and how I would be. I seemed to trigger him more than ever. I finally told him I was worried about him and thought he should see someone. I was actually concerned he might have a stroke or a heart attack, because when he got angry it seemed as though it was damaging his body. It was like he was trying to control his anger, but it wasn't working. He saw one therapist (mentioned earlier) who said he had anger issues and gave him a method of looking at what he was angry about and how to disperse it, but then Mada came into our lives and he discovered what it was all about.

Mada's healing method (the Dalian Method, DM) to get to the unconscious is so gentle and quick. As long as you bring along a willing heart and a courageous spirit to heal, she will lead you where you need to go and hold your hand until you're ready for her to let go. Trevor had the courage and trusted her enough to let her take him on the journey into his unconscious to discover what was there. By bringing awareness into our own unconsciousness, we not only heal ourselves, but effect all those who we come into contact with.

Mada explains she is working with Epigenetics. This is a field of energy that surrounds us and where our blocks are stored. These blocks have come from our conditioning and became our beliefs and our wounds. She is able to access this energy and bring it to our awareness, so we can transform it. Her work with Trevor helped him release this energetic block from his body and allowed him to heal his fear of abandonment. Exposing this energetic block is referred to as transforming the unconscious into consciousness. When you identify a physical pain, you breathe into that pain, express the emotion, and go deeper inside to see what you are holding onto. After identifying blocks, Mada shows you how to release them.

Before, Trevor didn't know this energy block was running in him. One could go to a therapist and talk, even recognize what happened and grieve, but it's the next step Mada takes that actually releases the block from your body. She has you breathe into your belly and out through different parts of your body, all the while repeating the beliefs she has identified that are running in your energy and aren't true but which you currently hold to be true. Then, she courageously helps you to see they are just old patterns and aren't you. She helps you transform your programming using the truth of who you are, which in turn empowers you instead of holding you as a victim to out-dated beliefs that aren't serving you any longer. You can actually feel this energy leave your body. These energetic blocks we carry around need to be identified and released. Otherwise, they become how we act in our lives and we remain stuck in old patterns. This isn't who we are; it's how we have been programmed. Most of us haven't any idea we have these programs running in us. We say: "That's just who I am, it's my personality." What makes us go looking? Struggle, depression, illness, unhappiness. We aren't taught how to release energetic blocks: we're not even aware that we have them. In many meditations, we are told to sit and go within to find stillness, but how can we find stillness if we don't even know what that feels like? Do we even know what it means to be conscious? It always feels as though we are trying to move "stuff", emotions and thoughts out of the way just to reach the stillness. Maybe we should go into the "stuff" first. There are, of course, other modalities that identify and release blocks. However, through traditional talk therapy it would seem that instead of erasing the causes of programs and the programs themselves (eradicating them from your energy field) often the therapist seems to suggest replacing one program with another. This layers the good program on top of the bad one, which then can create more confusion because it still becomes frustrating and work for the mind to try to figure out which one to run. In addition to being effortless, what sets Mada's method apart is that it actually transforms unconsciousness into consciousness. By releasing the contradictory layers of beliefs, thoughts, and emotions in the body; you don't have to work out the new level of consciousness or a new way to be; it just becomes you. It's like magic, but there aren't any words to truly describe the experience.

After the session and workshop with Mada, my husband went for his pre-scheduled appointment with his therapist. At the end of his session, his therapist told him he could see something profound had happened to him and he didn't need to see him any longer. With Mada's help, Trevor brought light into the darkness of his fear of abandonment. Now fully understanding where it had come from, the fear was naturally transformed, just by bringing in the awareness of its presence. The energy trapped in his body was able to be released, along with the trigger and reactions. This is truly magical work.

Days later, as we chatted with friends and family about what happened with Trevor, the only way I could find to explain his dramatic shift was to say: "A spaceship landed, took him on board, gave him a lobotomy, and sent him back to me." Honest to God, there really is no explanation one can put into words to explain the magnitude of what happened on this day.

The amazing thing about Mada's work is that once you have brought in consciousness on an issue, you don't have to train yourself how to be in this new way. You don't have to work at it because you're different. Other people will surely notice the change in you, even if you don't realize the change. For instance, when I had changed back to myself, I just knew I didn't have to retrain myself. I just had to figure out how to explain this to Trevor. So once you become aware of the patterns you were operating under and release them from your body, you can relax into the truth of who you've always been.

As I see it, Eckhart Tolle's books *The Power of Now* and *A New Earth* did a great job in paving the way for me to understand the ego and the importance of finding my inner stillness. He has a way of explaining what the ego is and why it's so important to recognize it. He reaches many people on a level they can understand through their minds, which is where most of us are operating from. With this understanding, we're now ready to comprehend Mada's message: the need to transform the unconscious running within us into consciousness to fully heal. As she says, before we are able to let it go we must first heal our "wounded ego" into a "healthy ego" and awaken into full consciousness. Mada's work takes you out of the mind and into your body and heart. I see this as the final step to transformation and healing. Consciousness is the key to health and happiness and Mada's practical method transforms unconsciousness into consciousness without the need to struggle for years with unnecessary pain and suffering. She believes if thousands of people use her technique to help heal themselves into consciousness, there will be enough explosive energy of consciousness to heal the collective pain and suffering on the entire planet! This is her commitment, passion, and life's work.

In her book, *In Search of the Miraculous*, Mada says: "The Earth is suffering because we are suffering." That's why becoming conscious is so important. It's a win-win situation, because when we heal on an individual level it is contributing to the global healing for our world. The only reason to resist becoming conscious is the fear of change, losing something you held so close and for so long even if it makes you sick. The ego is always trying to protect you, but what it doesn't realize is the thing it doesn't want to let go of is the very thing compromising your life and ability to be free, healthy and happy. It seems the saying: "Better the devil you know than the one you don't" is a belief many live by, even when it makes you unhappy and sick, is crazy. I understand though, because for me what I didn't want to let go of was so strong and engrained in my being at times I would rather suffer than heal. Sometimes it all seemed just too hard. I think that's why people give up, it's just easier to keep the peace and sacrifice their own happiness. Well, I'm here to tell you that this work is so worth it. What you think is hard is only a belief in your mind, it's not real, and this is the part that's hard to get over. Once you do, it's all down stream from there, so I encourage you to go for it. The fear you feel is an emotion. Breathe and do it anyway, step into your courage, go in and transcend your fears.

FEAR is a very powerful form of control - yet the only way past fear is to be courageous enough to feel it and realize it doesn't have a hold on you; you only believe it does and that gives it the power. Use fear as the engine, not as the brake. When most people start to "feel," they get scared and want to do or take something to stop that feeling. Trust yourself or if you are with someone you trust, and who has the courage to be there for you, then go into the fear even though it feels awful because there is insight awaiting you and just by doing this you will disperse the power it had over you and uncover the truth of what it was.

Mada says in her book: "Love, happiness and peace can't be found outside. To find these things we must let go of what blocks them - our ego mind. If we try to fix something on the outside, instead of knowing who we are from the inside, we continue to suffer."

CHAPTER TEN

Sins as a Mother

⁓

Song: "Forever Young" by Rod Stewart

The next time I went to see Mada was to get help when my son went through his divorce. It all started in July 2009 with the perfect wedding. Something went wrong and I needed some answers and I knew she would help me find them. As I sat in her Vancouver home, I told her what had happened to our son and that I didn't understand why it was affecting me so deeply.

It had been a fairy tale wedding set in the garden of our son's home on a perfect summer's day in July 2009. A big white tent had been set up, blue tablecloths with white china had all been laid out on the tables, blue-and-white balloons floated high over the tables, and flowers were everywhere. A hundred guests were arriving to witness this special day. The bride rode in on horseback wearing a beautiful white gown, her long veil and two small dogs trailing behind while a country-music song played in the background. Everything seemed right.

A few months later it all shattered when our son's wife decided to go away for extra job training. Initially, her idea was to take the training for the experience; however, a few weeks into the course she was clearly showing signs of enjoying herself and planning to take a job that had been offered to her. It became obvious she didn't want to come back or be with our son any longer. Perhaps they got married too soon?

I'd experienced drama in my life before, but nothing like this. Our son was devastated, as was I. I tried to help him by saying everything would be okay, but clearly it wasn't going to be. This led to weeks of emotional trauma, fear, anxiety, and exhaustion for my son, our family, and me. Her training took place in another province, so correspondence was through phone calls, emails, and texts, which weren't very clear. She seemed to be working all the time, so it was hard for our son to get any answers. We were completely thrown off by her behaviour. How could this be happening? Many events occurred during this time that I don't wish to discuss in this book, but let's just say it was extreme drama for several months.

Their wedding photos had just come back from the printers and were spread around their home. What was he supposed to do with them now? Hide them; throw them away? What about the gifts, and the video of the wedding? God, words couldn't explain the pain in my heart. My son said to me: "How will I ever be able to get over this and how can I ask our family to go through this again for me if and when I meet someone else?" His shame and embarrassment were overwhelming. My heart went out to him. I was in uncharted water - this was beyond my control. I always knew how to make him feel better, but not this time. This affected me deeply, perhaps even more so than anyone could have ever known and I didn't know why, at least not until later on. My son's wife had made a choice, now it was left to him to accept her decision.

Eventually over the next four months he found his own way to come to terms with the events and he filed for a divorce. Although the ordeal wasn't happening to me, somehow it felt worse; I had to watch my son in so much pain, which was sheer torture. That's where the mothering line seemed to get murky. What was my job in all of this? Did I need to fix it so I could feel better; even though my mind was trying to convince me I was helping our son? This was a big question and difficult to answer. I couldn't stand watching my son suffering. Interesting how I was recognizing that "I" again – "I" couldn't stand watching my son suffer. Is that why I needed to gain control of the situation, to help me feel better? It felt like I'd been through an earthquake. At one point, it was as though the earth below me had fallen away and I had been set adrift into the abyss of the unknown. I can honestly say I had never felt like this before. I wondered if this was what depression felt like. My mind seemed void, empty of thoughts; I didn't care about myself or anyone else for that matter. As the months went on, it was even hard to be there for my son. Sometimes he would call looking for some comforting answers, of which I had none. In the past, I had always been able to find my ground. I'd pick up an inspiring book or go for tea with a friend, but I didn't have any energy or urge to do either. I felt completely empty. What was going on with me? The actions of my son's wife went beyond our ability to understand. How was I ever supposed to help him understand when I surely didn't? As a mother you think you can figure out anything for your kids to help them, but not this time. I was having as hard a time with this as my son, and as I was to discover later, for different reasons.

I told Mada what had happened and that I was back to see her to make sure that I wasn't carrying any negative energy around with me still with relationship to this situation, I didn't want it showing up later in my life as some illness, I wanted to make sure I was clear of it all. She was able to see my energy was all over the place (out, not down), so it was hard to ground it. There was a lot of fear in me and I didn't understand where it was coming from. As in my first session, she saw "I had a fear to claim my power" from previous lifetimes of being punished. What did this have to do with my son's situation? It wasn't happening to me. She went on to say this was undermining my ability to stay grounded and do what needed to be done, "this belief is formed," she said, "through an experience from a past life."

In my case, it was deep in my unconscious. She told me in a past life I was crucified for standing up for myself and not just once: "So you have a belief in you that says, 'I better behave and I must not stand up or something will happen to me." That's where my fear was coming from, so I compromised. Mada said she could read there was also a belief in me that said: "I'm not good enough" from times in the past when people were burned at the stake. It still goes on today, she asserted, just in different forms about how society conditions people and cuts their roots to be tortured. "You start doubting yourself and the truth. You start to think maybe I am wrong, so I'm better if I just do what they want." It's a subtle hypnosis. The wiser the soul, the more you're attacked. Society doesn't want you to stand up; it's all about power. If you know more than they do, they are afraid of your power – "they" being anyone who is trying to keep you small and quiet and controlled.

On a deeper physical level, she continued, I had another belief running in me: "The masses are right and I'm wrong." If the masses said something I wasn't, I thought they were right and I was wrong. I needed to stand in my own truth, given I knew in my heart my intentions were good. She said: "That to be able to sing my own song, all truth seekers must break through this!" Trevor has helped me in this lifetime to do this just by being him. So, still running in my unconscious was, I don't trust myself. "We had to remove that," she said, otherwise, I would be stuck in a continuous loop and would never be able to find my grounding. To come out of the loop, I needed to take action. I needed to face my insecurity and jump. Unless I jumped, how would I know I was okay, that I was still alive and whatever I was afraid of it wasn't going to happen? It seemed this was my next step.

During the session, Mada also told me I trusted someone in a past life who was unconscious and he chopped off my head. No wonder I was so afraid to stand in my own power! All this stuff wasn't quite what I was used to hearing or delving into, but

I was open, I needed help, and I trusted her. I couldn't deny that everything was starting to make sense and now I knew why all of this had to happen to our son and me. The thread of *I don't trust myself and I can't stand up for myself* was running not only in me but in my son too. Was he the catalyst that was to finally help me step into my own self? Was this whole drama all part of the universal plan to help us evolve? Both of us?

As I see it, we run the risk of staying blinded to all of who we are if we think walking this Earth in this lifetime is all there is or ever was.

Mada went on to say I needed to watch myself because in my fear I needed to be in control. "Breathe into your belly, exhale out of your third eye," she continued, "Looking at the other side of the duality, how do we learn? We have an experience, we learn what our parents do and we do the same thing. We watch how someone in authority does something and we do it, too. If you're punished, you start believing maybe I'm wrong and they are right, then you start behaving like them, you adopt their beliefs so you start behaving the same way." She said my son's wife was only acting from what she learned growing up; she did what she saw other people in authority do and took control when she got scared. To come out of the duality, both parts of my personality needed to be recognized. She clarified: "This is how the mind works and you need to realize that you do this, too, and stop." I was in reaction with my son's wife; fear and control yo-yoed back and forth. "Look at the controlling part of yourself," Mada advised: "which works the same way as your persecutors did to you. Now you did that to her so until you recognize that, it can't stop." I get it, I replied. I really did. The more I learned about my beliefs, the more open I became to stop defending them.

My son's wife and I had had some challenges during this time, but before she left for her new job and life I managed to resolve things with her. I told her about my session with Mada and she could see the dynamics between us. Now, I knew I had to forgive her and myself for the events that took place. Otherwise, what would that say about what I had come to know as the truth? Even though the situation happened to my son, I still needed to respect that this was a woman who didn't feel as though she had a choice in her life and couldn't say "no" in a way that would be heard and okay, she didn't feel that she could speak her truth. Instead, perhaps she handled things the only way she knew how. How could I condemn her for that? If I did, then I would be condemning myself. Throughout all the months it took to work through my son's pain and mine, I realized why this was all happening. I didn't teach him to say "no", I didn't teach him to stand up for himself, because I didn't. He learned by watching me, just as I had learned by watching my mother. The awareness of this threw me into a determination like I'd never felt before; this would be my final attempt at changing this pattern within me with a hundred percent dedication. If I couldn't start speaking my truth and sticking up for myself, how the hell could I expect my children to? After this realization, I immediately started taking action and sticking up for myself, speaking my truth.

I was diligent in my mission to do and say everything I had always wanted to. I verbalized all I had suppressed, which was liberating and freeing. I didn't care how it made me look to others. I needed to get the truth of my thoughts out into the open of what they were doing from inside my head. I did this believing it was for my son, because I really thought if I didn't, he would have stayed in pain and I couldn't stand that. There's the "I" again, I couldn't stand my pain. So often we do things believing they are for others when, in fact (as I discovered), it is more often so we can relax and feel better all in the name of others. Knowing this today stops me from interfering in situations I have no place being. The hidden gift was: because I had to do it for myself first, both of us came out stronger human beings who trusted ourselves and could say no when we wanted to. It was a very tough but rewarding journey.

If you are being asked to step into all of you for yourself, you may find many different reasons not to, your mind plays tricks on you, and you chicken out and perhaps never become your authentic self. I changed believing it would help my son; therefore, I didn't even have those mind-chattering thoughts to talk me out of it. The voice in my head said: "You have to do this for you, or your son will never be able to, you have to show him how." I really believe this was the voice of my higher power, my true self, who is never afraid of anything, the voice of universal truth. People would say to me during those tough days: "You'll see Chenty, this will turn out to be a gift for you and your son." Even though part of me knew this was true, I still didn't want to hear that, but indeed it was a gift in the end.

At least two years prior to my son getting married, I went to see another psychic, a man from my sister's spiritual church. She was studying to be a minister and when she told me about him, I was interested. Emotionally, at that time I was letting go of my sister and my niece and I was completely fatigued. What he told me, which really ticked me off, was that he could see my son was going to go through a thorny time. He even said he might make a terrible mistake. "Your son sees roses, but it's a bad situation, it's thorny. You will want to rip off your nails [a good visual] when it happens and interfere, but don't. You can be there to support on the sideline, but you can not and must not interfere, this is his journey. He needs to feel the thorns himself. He's an innocent, it takes him a while to get things re: people's intentions, he trusts but when he gets it he really gets it. He's a great kid and it will work itself out in the end." The psychic also told me my son has, "my head on his shoulders, will be good at business, has a big heart, and admires his sister ." Of course, this was before my son's marriage and it didn't dawn on me that this was the thorny event until I remembered this session and got out my notes after his marriage was over.

In the session with Mada, I was finally going to understand why my son's divorce was so hard on me. I learned I had a karmic connection with my daughter-in-law to deal with in this lifetime. This was a huge part of the treatment and answered a lot of questions for me about why I was so attached to this situation and why it was so painful for me: it was a deep in-my-gut pain. I learned that in a past life I had trusted my daughter-in-law and she betrayed me. The karma in this lifetime was for me to be able to see trusting an unconscious person is dangerous because he or she is asleep and therefore not aware of his or her actions. This was huge for me. I used to believe if I loved someone enough I could help that person wake up, but indeed I can't. No one can help another to wake up unless that person chooses to and some never do. I learned to "stand in my own power" and not put myself in harm's way anymore. The only way to help another wake up is to "be true to you". The reason my daughter-in-law was connected to me in this lifetime was for me to release her from this past-life experience, so she could move forward and on with her journey in life and for me to do the same. This was profound for me. It really helped me, my patterns changed and I relaxed. Concurrently, I think differently about where I fit in this life and where I stand on "helping" people. I wasn't bound to Christian conditioning any longer, which played a big role in the way I used to think.

Since then, I feel much more grounded and peaceful, but a little sad for the loss of my daughter-in-law. Still, I know existence has a plan for her, so I trust in that. I feel as though I have come through the darkness of the unknown into the light. My desire and need for the truth led me to seek out others who would help me figure it all out. No wonder it was so hard and I was so confused and so afraid. To be able to understand the karmic connection between my daughter-in-law and myself was huge to me. During Mada's session, I truly felt the connection and healing. I don't question why this had to happen to my son, because I now know. I'm not sure if I would have ever stepped into my true self had this hadn't happened and perhaps neither would have my kids. One of the hardest things to do is to let go and I was able to once having the understanding. My stumbling point was always: "I can help". I thought I knew better for her and what she needed, when, in fact, how could I? I didn't know anything about her. I just had to trust that to let her go was the kindest thing I could do.

My son also had a session with Mada during this difficult time and he learned "not to compromise himself for the love of another". I truly believe if he hadn't had this session, he wouldn't have been able to handle this situation as well and maturely as he did. After meeting with Mada I could see the difference in him. Not right away but a few weeks later when his wife returned home to collect her things; he was different with her. Instead of fear there was a confidence that enveloped him. He stood tall, firm, and grounded, unlike me at that time. There was a moment when I was freaking out and for the first time he spoke firmly but calmly to me saying he had it all under control; I wasn't to worry and for me to go home. Suddenly, the tides had turned: I wasn't the mother with all the wisdom and answers for her son any longer. Instead, he had become his own person, tapping into his inner wisdom and I could feel it. He was empowered.

Remarkably he has moved forward and is once again back to his naturally happy state of being. I know he won't "compromise himself" again for the love of another. Mada pointed out to him he said, "Yes" when he meant "No". I taught him well. His conditioning (me) led him to believe if he said no, he would be met with anger and judgment and because he didn't like confrontation, he opted for yes more than no, going against his true self. So really, thank God it all happened in the end … and yes, my friend was right. I did end up seeing the gift it brought to both of us.

Without Mada's help I know I would have been drifting around in the unknown of this for a long time and who knows how much more damage I would have caused to myself or others, emotionally or physically by internalizing the pain and the fear I felt. Her work is ground breaking and takes talk therapy to a whole new level. I could have talked for months and never would have reached what I did with her in that one-and-a-half-hour treatment.

I have discovered that it's in my ability to watch myself and become a witness to my actions with detachment from my wounded ego that has enabled me to see my own unconsciousness in action. This means not judging the events or actions of my life as good or bad, they're just events. I don't say this lightly. It really is what I have come to know and allows me to investigate what, why, and how things happen in my life. Everything is for my higher self to emerge. I now know I always have a choice in how to respond to events, without shame, blame, judgment, or any other kind of suppressing emotions. It's an acceptance of what's happening because it needs to at this time. There's a treasure to find with the awareness, the ability to watch myself while I'm actually in process with another or even just myself. In other words, to look down on a conversation or events happening as if I'm floating above and just watch, being able to be detached from the situations, which in turn means the ego doesn't get involved and if and when it tries to - I'm on it. I can see what it's trying to do, gain control, then I can stop it, because I know the need to gain control is a result of being in fear and I have been triggered by my own wounded ego. It's a false reality; I can breathe and let it go, knowing all will be fine. It's just an old wound surfacing.

I love being the detective of my own life.

This brings to mind passages I once read from the book called, *Awakening into Oneness: The Power of Blessing in the Evolution of Consciousness* by Arjuna Ardagh:

"While the early claims for a state of permanent enlightenment sounded like an arrival, Bhagavan speaks of the crossing of the threshold in the brain as the beginning of an endless process."

"Enlightenment is the first step. It is the beginning of the real journey. First you get an enlightened state, a peak experience, which has to result in enlightenment sooner or later. After that it is a never-ending process. The process ultimately stops only when you merge into light. Until then it goes on and on. It will go on while you are on this planet. After you've left the planet, it still continues. There is no end to it."

He compares the mind to a boxing match, where different personalities are always in conflict with one another. Before any kind of an awakening you feel like you are inside the ring, getting punched continually, from every side. When the brain passes through the thresholds mentioned above, you step out of the ring. The conflict continues, but you now know that it's not happening to you. As the brain continues to shift, the process deepens, and even the fighting can become less frequent. Then one day, the boxers finally stop fighting, sit down together, and have tea. Then the ring itself disappears and there is absolute stillness."

I love these observations as they explain the constant conflict with the ego, but also that one day it is possible to reach peace and enter into a state of grace.

In my writing group many years ago, I wrote this poem:

Grace
Stillness is when I'm soaring up
Grounded yet free
Interwoven, like the earth and the sky
Do I go to the end, will I fall?
I must trust, all will be as it should be
Grace hides around every corner look out for it!
Unloved, undernourished, no one to care for it
Reality, is any of this real? Or am I the only one?
What is happening to me?
Grace
Stillness is when I'm soaring up
Grounded yet free
Interwoven like the earth and the sky, connected
Do I go to the end, will I fall?
I must trust, this is all a process
Everything is as it should be
Grace

When I listen to how people are experiencing reality, then I see it. I realize they are getting caught up in things I can't imagine being part of. That is the state of grace, the ability to just be.

CHAPTER ELEVEN

Around The World on Two Wheels

Song: "If Today was Your Last Day" by Nickelback

After our son's divorce was finalized in the spring of 2010 and our children were once again doing well, it was time for me to reflect and let my body catch up to all I'd learned in the past few years. I was tired and had lost interest in my accounting work. I felt as though there must be more for me to do and give, so I asked the universe, what should I do?

One March day I found myself in my office staring at my computer wondering why I was there and why my brain wouldn't function properly. At one point I even thought there might be something seriously wrong with me, but looking back I knew I was done with this job and needed to realize this. Sitting inside those four walls day after day staring at a computer screen just didn't feel like enough anymore. I wanted to be of greater service. Each one of my sisters had found work in which they were giving something back and I wanted to give back too. I'd had a successful career in our construction company for the last thirty years and felt it was time for something different.

Trevor still wasn't sure how the recent events had taken its toll on us. He was still fragile from all my revelations. He was trying to catch up and understand who I had become. Yet, all he wanted to know was, where ever I was going, would we still be together?

We had been in our new home for several months and I really thought this was where we would stay for quite some time. It had the acreage and privacy I wanted. Trevor was planning to buy a tractor and I wanted a horse, but it wasn't meant to be. I was at home one afternoon when it came to me, what about a trip around the world on our motorcycle? We had both watched the DVD's called: *A Long Way Round* and *A Long Way Down* about two guys who went around the world on their BMW motorcycles. We loved their adventures and had often said that one day we would do that too. As I mentioned earlier, Trevor had always wanted to go around the world on a sailboat, but that wasn't for me. Now a bike, that could work at least I could get off whenever I wanted. I could sit on the back, listen to my music, and watch the world go by. I could spend some time in my own head and reflect on all that had happened. Trevor could ride the bike, which is what he loved to do. This could be a win-win idea. I wasn't attached to my new home; with our construction business we had renovated and sold houses many times before.

When Trevor came home that evening from work, I suggested perhaps it was time to do just that. Of course, he thought it was terrific and he couldn't believe I would be suggesting such a thing. Then his mind went to how could we afford this and I said: "Let's sell the house." The truth is, we hadn't even got around to figuring out all the electronic equipment in the house yet (an advanced sound system with iPods in every room) or even how the new fridge or coffee machine worked. Though the adventure might be complicated, I didn't care. It seemed so freeing just to get on the bike and ride.

We both knew we had to be fit enough to ride a motorcycle around the world so the timing was right - we had both been going to a personal trainer and doing strength exercises. From then on we started planning when we would go and where, how would we get the bike around the world, and how much would it cost. We talked to our business partners, our brothers and sisters, and given our good relationship they understood and were okay with it. We put the house on the market and to our surprise it sold within six weeks, which rarely happens on our small island. Houses often take years to sell here, so we saw this as a sign we were doing the right thing. In trade we took a small, one-bedroom house and it was perfect. It had a fantastic view and a double car garage to store our things while we were away.

We set our budget at CAD$200 a day, which had to include all our personal expenses and the bike, so this wasn't going to be a cheap trip. I was still really tired during all this planning and wasn't much help. I just wanted to go and didn't really care where at that point. My mind was clear and full of possibilities, but my body was still trying to catch up, particularly my adrenals, which hadn't yet recovered.

We had a lot to do. We had to pack up our stuff, get our finances in order, and figure out how to transport the bike around the world: our biggest concern and cost. It turned out the bike needed its own passport called a "Carne De Passage"; along with a hefty deposit should we not return to Canada with it. I also wanted to make sure the kids would be okay; we had leaned on one another heavily through our son's divorce and now it was time to let go and start enjoying life again. When we went to the doctor to make sure we were healthy; however, both Trevor and I had strange counts in our blood results, particularly Trevor. It was serious enough for our doctor to suggest that we postpone the trip to book other appointments months in the future. We looked at each other and agreed we didn't want to wait; we were going to see the world. It was an adventure that in itself would be healing.

On April 30, 2010, a month before we were due to leave on our trip, I was sitting in our newly renovated one-bedroom home packing when I felt the need to write Trevor a letter. I had changed and although I felt good, I was tired, but he was still confused by the new changes and me he was seeing in my behaviour. I could tell he was worried. I never gave him the letter. The first time he read it was in this book two years later after we got back. I guess I was still too afraid back then, I wasn't quite sure if he was ready to hear what was in it. Still, it was my truth, this much I knew. Sharing my thoughts with others has always embarrassed me, as though they were odd or weird and people would judge me. As a result I kept them to myself most of the time, few seemed to understand me. Even today, when I go on Facebook to write a comment I'm very aware to not say something casual unless it's coming from my truth and I'm prepared to take responsibility for it.

My letter to my hubby was as follows:

April 2009 Love doesn't ask why
Trevor:
My heart is big; my heart is deep and expansive. I have enough love for the whole world over. Never think my love diminishes for you just because I have enough for the world. Never think you are not special to me, you are the one who keeps me tethered to this ground, for I have always wondered if I might just take flight one day, but I have a deep knowing I am supposed to be here with you and I am to stay on this ground. Yes, it may be my desire for myself to take flight, but that is not what I came here to do. Perhaps I live in two worlds, but I am clear about being here in this world in this lifetime.

So I do understand where your fear comes from. I understand when you say there may not be a place for you and that you worry you are trying to keep up with me and worry about being left behind. I do understand that fear.

But you need to hear me when I say you don't need to worry. I know my life as it is, is exactly where it is meant to be. I don't doubt that in our future I will be doing something in the healing field. It may be to write a book and do lectures, I don't know the answer, but I'm asking you to just trust you will always be in my life. I want you in my life, you bring me laughter, you love me to bits, you are strong and beautiful. I know because of who I am, I am not easy to understand or live with because of my passion for love of the world, but I want you to know I chose you because I believe you have the same passions as me and because I never doubt your love for me or my love for you. I also understand it has to be your choice to be with me.

The anger I'm seeing in you is your fear of losing me. I understand that, but I'm asking you to trust this is not going to happen, so your fear can stand down because we both want the same thing from each other. You might be saying to yourself, 'No it's not that, it's that I am not enough for you,' but it breaks down to the same thing. We are both hard to love because of who we are. I, because of my life passion, and you, because you don't believe you are lovable or are worthy of love given you were not shown this as a child, so in our own way we both feel we are hard to love.

What I want to know is when everyone else in the world doesn't understand me, that you always will; when I am sad because I don't understand me, that you will be there to hold me and say you do; when I am afraid, you will tell me it's all going to be okay; when you are angry at me for not doing what you want me to do, that you will soften your tone and realize it's just your ego in fear of never having enough and hold me and say I'm sorry; when I am happy that you will be there to share the laughter; when I need to be alone it is you who understands and gives me my space from a safe, loving place in your heart, for whatever my needs are; that you will understand and allow me to be me without the fear of being left behind.

When you put your arms around my waist, it speaks to me that you love me. I know I have a good body and look good for my age, because you keep telling me that part. What I don't know is do you see me, do you love me even though I am hard to love, can you love me the way I am? This task I have chosen in my life, my passion for world peace and for all humans to understand love is the only way, this is who I am. I realize it comes with people who don't understand or appreciate me, but that is what I have chosen to be. I believe in a past life I have been killed for my deep concern and love for others, so for me to fully embrace it in this lifetime has been difficult and takes courage because I was afraid of being ostracized, people (their egos) are afraid of what they feel from me and I have to live with that, which is why people lash out at me sometimes—family, friends, etc. I can accept and live with all of that with you in my life, because I know you know I come from love, but without you in my life, I may be alone. You are a rare breed that is strong enough and confident enough to be with me. You have a deeper knowing your ego is trying to keep you from, which is that you are lovable and you are loved.

You may think I'm talking about myself here, but that's the thing, you and I are more alike than you realize. We are peas in a pod and I believe with the absence of fear in our lives, we can be the two happiest, luckiest people on this planet and fulfill our wildest dreams, and as you told Nige, share your world, share your passions, and you will inspire others.

So let's go on this trip and just have fun, with no expectations of each other and leave the fears at home.

If this doesn't get you to believe or hear how much I love you, then it's just that you aren't yet in a place to be able to hear me and hopefully one day soon you will.

I offer what you cannot buy—devoted love until you die.

I love you, Me

The weekend before we were due to leave, one of my sisters had a big going away party for us at her beautiful home and the whole family, along with all our friends, came to wish us well. I remember feeling quite surreal knowing I was there, but observing myself at the same time, happy I was going off on this big adventure. A niece decided to make a bet I would be home within a short period of time, because I would be fed up with the trip. She even got others involved in posting bets as well. It was understandable, given the events during our last motorcycle trip to Europe the previous year. I guess they thought I wouldn't be able to handle it, but I had changed since then. I didn't think I would cut the trip short, but after what I'd been through I didn't really know what to expect or how long I would enjoy it. I just knew I needed to go. Everyone in my family knew what I had gone through with our son's divorce earlier that year and that I was tired, yet perhaps they didn't really know me anymore and how I'd changed.

We left for our adventure on my birthday, May 30, 2010: from living on our little island to travelling around the world on two wheels. It would be fourteen months and thirty countries later before we would return home. Our daily blog documenting the trip is called: "It's a Long Way Somewhere" (see Author's Page) which became our joint new jobs. Trevor would take photographs and I would write the text. Perhaps one day this will also become a book.

It was days and days of long straight roads as we headed east across Canada; miles and miles of farmland; the smells of on coming summer; and rolling fields of wheat. I was aware I wasn't yet in my happy place, I was just observing day after day. I watched people in these small towns go about their days and wondered what they were thinking and what their lives were really like. I felt a bit cynical as we passed by them and I wondered why my thoughts were negative. I could sense Trevor knew I wasn't quite right, but he never said much. I think he knew I was recovering from the life I'd been living in the last few years, how it had taken its toll on me and perhaps I just needed time.

As we continued east we stayed in motels and spent the evenings planning the next day's route. Our idea was to ride as far east as we could to Bar Harbour, Maine, in the United States and then back to Montreal. From there, we'd fly to Ireland, ride through Scotland and England, over to Europe and who knows where else as we made our way around the world.

I remember one night in Sault Ste Marie, Northern Ontario, while we were waiting to cross the street a homeless man struck up a conversation with us. I was glued to his words as he told us he was waiting for his angel. I thought, oh yeah, but then he went on to talk about love and how it's just a word we all use too easily without really knowing what it means. He told us what's really required is respect, what he believed to be mostly missing in our relationships. I thought, hmm he's right, if you have respect between the two of you, this brings with it the true meaning of loving someone. Smart guy, random conversation, yet I never forgot him. He would be just one of many wise souls we bumped into along our ride who would either say something profound, invite us into their homes, or share a cup of tea with us right along the roadside. These were magical moments on our trip.

In Quebec we'd checked into a hotel for the night in the small town of Perce, on the Gaspé Peninsula. I didn't feel much like planning the next day's events that evening. I was just happy to be and do nothing. I think I was still suffering from adrenal fatigue. When I look back at the photos of me taken during that time, I look flat, expressionless, and sad. It frustrated Trevor that I wasn't interested in the planning. He wanted me to join in and be part of it. He was disappointed in me for not helping or showing any interest. I told him I didn't feel like it, I wanted to be left alone with my own thoughts. Once again, this wasn't anything how I used to behave. What could he do? He had to accept my wishes. I wasn't even sure why I was feeling this way.

This turned out to be the last time we had a conflict in which I had to say exactly what I needed without him trying to change my mind. Normally I would have felt bad and do what he wanted, thinking I was in the wrong, but not anymore. My life had changed - forever.

From that day on, I continued speaking out and saying what I wanted and felt. Concurrently, I listened to what he wanted, and then we would come to an agreement. After that point it wasn't hard; finally, Trevor understood that I too should be able to speak my truth. I had come to understand the saying: "divorce the story, marry the truth". I had delved into my belief system and conditioning and found out where it originated and now I chose to continue my life with a new set of beliefs that were, indeed, my own. I realized I had created my own reality: by what I believed and by my fears. I had lived my life in protection and now I was living it exposed and vulnerable - now I was alive and free of the fear to be me.

Shortly after on June 27th, we celebrated our 29th wedding anniversary. We stayed in a lovely boutique hotel in the great little town of Tadoussac, Quebec. I hadn't bought Trevor a card, but I sat him on the bed before we headed down for dinner and asked him to put one bud of my iPod in his ear and I put one in mine. Céline Dion's, "The Colour of My Love," was playing and although he doesn't normally listen to Céline Dion, the words were ones I wanted him to hear. They said everything I felt deep within my heart, better than any card I could have found. I thought how gentle and in love with love Céline seemed to be. Her lyrics explode the emotions of love, with words such as: "I offer what you cannot buy, devoted love until you die". (I wanted to print out the whole song in this book; however, stringent copyright laws don't allow for that so check the lyrics out on You Tube or my website, please see my author's page.)

I was finally able to love freely with an open heart because I was able to love myself.

The following month as I sat in Montreal's airport awaiting our flight to Ireland, thoughts drifted in my head once again about what it means to really love someone and the words to another song by Céline Dion came to mind: "If you give your soul to me, will you give too much away?"

I'm sure this is a question many of us worry about in our relationships. When we fall in love, it is a free feeling of endless possibilities and excitement mixed with shyness and polite respect. We never really know where it will lead, so we don't say or do too much. We just wait and see, not expecting anything, and it's enough if we are pleasantly surprised. Then, over time we seem to lose that feeling. It's hard to explain why and where it goes and we may ask, can it return again? We blame life, family, jobs, money, and so many things, but we have become full of expectations and we have lost the respect for one another: just as the man at the crosswalk in Sault Ste. Marie said.

Does the question come back to: "Is what we are really afraid of: being vulnerable, being exposed, really being seen for who we are and giving our soul away?" We are the protectors of our soul and if we're brave enough to expose it, will it be treated gently and with love? Do we keep it covered tightly just in case and never really know true love? Do we spend most of our lives in protection? The answer for me was yes, I had, but not any longer. I didn't want to just survive. I wanted to live to my life's fullest potential. I wanted to be brave enough to put myself out there so I could know all of who I am, I didn't want to be afraid of being me any longer.

As I see it, to be able to love freely, we must be able to also receive freely. In our fear, do we adjust to situations and become less than honest? Does being honest mean perhaps not getting what we want or think we need? Perhaps this is a behaviour we learned growing up. Maybe at a young age we did trust and exposed our souls only to have them crushed and hurt, so they went into hiding. I do believe at birth we are open to loving and receiving love freely.

When we first meet, we have very little expectations because we know we haven't the right; and furthermore, we haven't any control. We don't want to rock the boat, so to speak, so we are consciously cautious: **conscious** being the key here.

Some will think about what I have just stated and assert: "I am honest." However, this requires us to really sit and ponder for a while, because it's very likely the true answer is - we aren't always honest. Usually we're afraid to be honest in case we don't get what we think we need or want. If you're brave enough, ask those you trust and love the question and see what they have to say about you, you may be surprised!

Do you have the courage to be wrong?

Recently I commented to my niece that to put an expectation on someone else is wrong. As I see it, if the person doesn't meet your expectations, then you will be annoyed and disappointed. It isn't fair to put your expectations on another. She came back to me quite strongly with: "Of course we have expectations. We have expectations of all kinds of things in life, like our parents, that they will love us and be there for us." Well, from my point of view some parents are able to be there and some can't, but is that their fault? And if we judge them isn't that harsh on our part when we don't know the facts? Is that love? She went on to offer other expectations: "When we are married we will be loved and treated with love, that our children will love us, and so on. When we go to the doctor he will help us, when we go to a restaurant we will get food, when we go to a bank they will give us money." I could see it was confusing, though it's always good to have another opinion. I should have clarified I was referring to relationships. I find one of the biggest problems in our world is that we have too many expectations of other people in our lives: in love, in business, in friendships, in relationships. And when people don't meet our expectations, we react. If we have an expectation, how can we truly love with an open heart?

In my relationship with my children for instance, I see them as individuals with their own journeys to travel. I will always love them no matter what and I never want to get in the way of the choices they make in their lives - even if I don't like or agree with them. I have learned enough to know I don't want to control things that aren't mine to control. It's not my job and furthermore, this isn't love.

I want to love with an open heart. I want to be brave enough to fully open and expose every corner of what my heart holds inside for all to feel and embrace before I die. I don't want to have an expectation of anyone I'm in a relationship with. Some may say: "I don't love," or "I don't care," but for me, no expectations equates unconditional love. It's really hard for some people to understand this, because they have been brought up with a strong sense of what is expected in life, relationships, parenting, marriage, friendships, and business. It's my belief if we could learn to be completely vulnerable and honest to speak our own truths, this would open up a whole new section of our own hearts.

In short: we're afraid. It's like the song says: "If you give your soul to me, will you give too much away."

I was guilty of this in my early life and relationships. I was brought up a good Catholic and my mother taught us to put ourselves last while making sure everyone else was happy first. We were always to make sure someone else got the biggest piece of cake; was first in the line; got to speak first; in other words, someone else was always more important. This was the message I got, so I lived this until a few years ago: until I was forty-nine years old. It's very strange to drop those beliefs and way to live. At first it felt wrong. People around me continued to make me feel bad because I had changed my behaviour, but after a while they got used to it and now it feels so good to believe in myself and understand that I matter too.

I grew up with the message: "I had to compromise myself for the love of another" Yuk, Yuk, Yuk - that is so not true and this is the Christian conditioning. Yes, I believe Jesus sacrificed his life for us, but it wasn't by "not mattering". As I see it, the Bible and religion got it all wrong. Jesus had a passion for spreading true love on this planet and he was prepared to die for it: I feel and believe as deeply as he did, but that's not what I was taught. From all of my Catholic teachings, the only thing that ever stuck with me was that Jesus walked the Earth with unconditional love, that's it. My belief in that it should be possible is what sent me on this journey.

In believing that "I don't matter", I became resentful for not living my life according to me and I became untruthful. I went underground; protecting my soul to get what I needed the only way I thought I could. I wanted to blame everyone else for "making me" behave this way, but now that I'm honest, I realize no one can make me do anything. I did it because this was the only way I knew how to get what I needed, be that to protect my soul or someone else's and to get peace. We do what we do because that's what we learned. There isn't any shame: it's the unconscious within us. However, once we have learned, we need to fess up and stop doing it. You'll gain a huge amount of respect and the bigger bonus - you'll live your life according to you and people will still love you.

Bringing in this awareness, is consciousness

Arriving in Ireland with the bike was as easy as leaving Canada. We took a cab over to the cargo bay at the Dublin Airport, waited an hour and then there it was. I tell you, it was like waiting for a baby to come out from an operation. It even brought a tear to my eyes, never mind Trevor's. This bike was about to become a very important part of our world.

Before we left Canada we had contacted people in the Dublin Motorcycle Club asking them if anyone would be interested in showing us around their country and to our surprise we had a number of responses. Damien was one of them. After spending a few days in Dublin and adjusting to the time difference, we arranged to meet him at a bridge on the east side of the city.

The first thing we did was go for a coffee and he introduced us to a family tradition. When a family member goes travelling, they are given a special gift. He handed each of us a little white box … and inside was a silver ring with the Trinity knot symbol. The significance of the endless Trinity Knot is well known to travellers and noted throughout history as it represents a journey (or The Journey) that hasn't an ending or a beginning, where its path is intertwined with the paths of others throughout, "The Journey of Life". How lovely is that? Inside the boxes was a poem written on scroll.

> The Travellers Prayer
> May the road rise up to meet you
> May the wind be always at your back
> May the sun shine warm upon your face
> And the rains fall soft upon your tracks
> And until we meet again
> May god hold you safely in the palm of his hand.

What a guy and what an honour. We were both very touched indeed and had big lumps in our throats: and we'd only just met Damien.

We loved Ireland with its wet green fauna, small winding roads and stacked stonewalls. This country is packed with historical sites, some much older than even the pyramids and it just has so much character. The Giant's Causeway, the tombs, the people, the food, the music, and the pub life fascinated me. This country turned out to be one of my favourite places. It brought me back to myself, for the first time in a number of years I started to feel whole again. I had recognised a feeling of coming back home to myself, it felt familiar and there was a sense of peace.

There is something so resilient about the Irish people. It seems the tougher the times; the closer people come together. There really is a sense of community. We were there at the time of the

Celtic Tiger, the economic downturn, but it didn't seem to crush the spirits of the Irish as the pubs were still alive with music. This trip was proving to be just what I needed.

Many years ago, a psychic had told me I was like an engine running on high revs and if I didn't slow down it wouldn't be good for my health. He said it in such a way that it scared me, as though it were a life and death thing. I had to change my life style, take better care of myself, and fill myself up. He said it would take three years to do this. "Go with your joy," he told me. All I would be giving up is someone else's fear. He advised me to tell Trevor that I was on the track to happiness and then he could be, too; as long as he didn't go into his own fears and I was to reassure him all would be good. He said Trevor trusted me, but he didn't see his fear was greater than the trust. The psychic finished by saying we would soon be going on a big adventure, so I guess he was right - about everything!

It was my ability to have faith that I could let go of the tight hold I had over myself, and my fears, that allowed my life to start flowing in the direction it wanted to go. It turns out on this trip I was to discover why I was here and my task in life. From my life experience I believe our gifts won't be discovered as long as we continue to protect and judge our selves, our lives and hold on so tight to our beliefs. We must learn to let go and let life flow in its natural path. I believe love is the silence in the heart, a moment when time is still.

As Albert Einstein said: "A human being is part of a whole, called by us the 'Universe' a part limited in time and space. He experiences himself, his thoughts, and feelings, as something separated from the rest - a kind of optical delusion of his consciousness. This delusion is a kind of prison for us, restricting us to our personal desires and to affection for a few persons nearest us."

As I see it, our task must be to free ourselves from this prison by widening our circles of compassion to embrace all living creatures and the whole of nature in its beauty.

The adventures continued as we travelled from Ireland to Scotland; from England over to Europe; dipped into Morocco back to Spain; over to France and Italy; ferried over to Greece and Turkey; into Syria, Jordan, and Egypt all just before the unrest broke out in those countries. My husband said I must have dropped some of my consciousness along the way and that's why those countries were changing ... hmm I don't think I had that much influence. We went from Egypt into Israel, which was another pleasantly surprising country that we loved along with its people, and then eventually we flew to India. From there we went to Nepal onto Thailand, through Laos, Cambodia, Malaysia, Singapore, flew onto Australia and then back home, but that's a whole other book.

Fourteen months on the back of our bike was just what I needed to rest my body and relax into the way of being away from all that I knew. I could now embody all of my new self. I noticed myself being more open and vulnerable, where as before I would sit back and let Trevor do the talking. I now came forward and was determined to be front and centre and take my place in the world.

CHAPTER TWELVE

Unconditional Love

ے

Song: "The Greatest Love of All" by Whitney Houston

I set out on this journey with three questions: Does unconditional love really exist? Why do I have a fear to speak my truth? And can I be me without losing you? I have found the answer to them all.

We are always learning: even after my fifty years of being alive and thirty-one of those years being married. I firmly believe every moment brings with it a new revelation. The real gift is to understand that we're spiritual beings having a human experience; this hasn't anything to do with religion. This truly allows us to detach from being human and being attached to others and the way they are. It's only when you have found unconditional love for yourself that you don't need others to behave in a certain way any longer and you don't blame them for your life situation. It's brilliant!

In the spring of 2012 I discovered Master Dhyan Vimal and his teachings. He is from Malaysia and I had the opportunity to attend the "I & I Discoveries" that augments "I won't influence you, thereby I earn the right not to be influenced by you." This is a difficult concept to grasp. If you really think about it, it seems like an impossible task. It isn't. It just takes real commitment. My husband believed everyone who has been enlightened is single and he wanted to know why this seemed to be the case. He wanted to know because if it's true, he doesn't want to become enlightened. I asked Master Dhyan Vimal, here is his answer.

"In a sense what your husband is saying is right, all enlightened people are single, but in this sense they are one, not split, they are one in nature. What is the within and the without is one, so they are not split, so your husband is right, and they are with themselves in rightness, they start not to need others in a way to keep an ego or a lie, but they love, and this is the key.

Most, even in the East, are afraid when someone starts to study and move in this, they believe that they will leave their family behind, and leave their love ones behind, and this has been there since Buddha, who left his wife and family and went to find enlightenment. So this fear is there, but this is a good question for me to put to rest, this lie and this fear.

For now most relationships are based on needs and it's usually anchored in the fear of losing this need. One can't be alone so one needs another, one wants another so one is looked after in case something happens, there is a body need, or a need to love and be loved, and then the other is needed. And all relationships based on needs are not real relationships, and this same need is what drives each other away, and know this, in need one is alone with one's need being filled and that is all the relationship is.

People who seek this are people who seek the ability to truly love, and to find their truth, which is love, and they love too, but this love is from personal mastery and meditation, and this love has no need, but all it does is just love. And only this kind of love can help one meet another, and when this kind of love meets another, one is not alone, one is with the other. So in a strange sense, people who come to love are the one that is not alone, they are with another in such a deep sense.

But this is hard to understand, for most relationships are based on need, and when one has no needs as such, then people start to think they are alone and will not be with another. So in some sense, this need is the relationship that all are in, and in knowing this most start to make being with another a trade, 'I give you this and you give me that', and there is always accounting, and fairness and this and that.

Love is the ability to be with another, if at all it has a need, the only need is to be, and to be with another that is all it is in freedom. When one comes to this path, one comes to it because there is a deep demand in them to be, to learn just to be, and to be is to love, and love acts, and one of the actions is to be with another.

Now Chental, let your husband know, that you are doing this to learn to be more, and in this being, you will be with him more, and it's the art of falling into love that you are learning. But also say that your aloneness is intact, and you have to realize that you are alone, which we all are, but the difference is you are not escaping it, you are entering it, and in that you are learning to be with another - in love.

Your husband must care for you deeply, and I think he wants to be with you, and this shows you are in the right environment in which you can grow, and enter deeper love with him, so his fear of you being enlightened and being single can be dropped.

In the East, when most become monks, one of the key reasons is to stop abusing relation for needs, and using the other to escape ones aloneness, but the whole work is to attain to love, a love that is without needs and abuse.

I love the image of Shiva, for he is a Hindu god, and he had a wife and children, and most Hindu gods had a family, and this is the right understanding, but the whole thing was missed when people think being alone is the highest thing in the name of spirituality, but this is a lie, when one enters the lesson of love, one wants to love and love for real and without abuse.

And this is my stand. To all my disciples, know that we are alone, but we don't have to be all alone, in our aloneness the other is, and one can be with the other, and this being with another is what real love is, it never destroys your aloneness, for that is your freedom too, but in that freedom there is love, and with love the other is too.

Just yesterday in the centre in Malaysia I was saying that people who think only they exist, and it's all about them, who just want all things to be about them and they don't believe anyone else exists, should be avoided in this place. For a long time I have met many people that come and it's always only about them, it's about their happiness or their success, and it's always only about them.

These people are an enemy to love, for in their reality the other has no room except to serve them, and it's only about them. Even in the name of meditation this has been done, but this is human error, not of meditation. This is the reason there is a sanggha, and seva is the highest I can teach anyone, and in this, the other is, and in that other one is too.

This world is mad in this sense, it has trained people to live only for themselves, and all else must serve them, and even in the East where this idea of seva and love has been established for so long is now being infected with this idea of self-serving mind and this is hell in the making.

Living for another, and living in a way the other is included is the way to live, and this is the work you are undertaking. Your enlightenment will include not only your husband but all of mankind, and that is the right way, all else is a misunderstanding, but it will not be in the base of need, but based on love.

And I can see that you are very lovable, and I am sure there is much love in your life, and know this is what is needed for you to grow, all else is just a worldly affair, and it's just for use, other than that nothing much can be said about it.

You have asked how to make your husband feel safer, well tell him the truth, and live in a way that you show you really want to be with him and that is what is your relationship is about, which is being with one another, and tell him what you are learning is to learn to do that better, and this comes by you healing in being you, and in being you, he is too.

Another thing that has to be known is that in a relationship, if you are sad, you bring sadness to the other too, if you are happy you bring this to other too, if you are enlightened you bring this to the other too and this the nature of being with one another, so in you working to awaken you, you awaken another. If I bless you, you husband is blessed too, so one is and the other is, and this is the key understanding.

Master DhyanVimal,
Founder, Friends to Mankind
February 2012
Thank you Master.

Unconditional love was hidden deep within my subconscious; I had to peel away all the layers of my conditioning to discover it hiding patiently waiting to be acknowledged again. I had finally remembered me, the saying comes to mind: "It's time to remember the truths, we have been conditioned to believe the lies."

In our lives we don't know why we do the things we do. I didn't know why it was so hard for me to receive and love myself until I went on this internal journey. The journey I went on is a natural cycle of our lives and seems to cause the most disturbance, but it ends up making us feel free to be who we are and to love on a much deeper level than ever before. Many of us never take this journey because we have been conditioned to believe it's selfish. Chogyam Trungpa said in his book, *Smile at Fear*, "You are a warrior when you have the bravery to face who you are, without fear, embarrassment, or denial. Learn to smile at fear."

Whatever you do, promise yourself one thing; that you will keep searching and uncover the layers of conditioning to find the real you. Don't believe the ego mind when it tries to tell you you're being selfish. I have proved that voice comes from our conditioning and the truth is we can only truly love another with our whole hearts when we can truly love ourselves first - so you see it's not selfish at all.

I spoke with a woman the other day and she labels the time in her life when she became a wife and a mother as the "invisible years". She knows she wasn't being one hundred percent herself, but she accepted life as she believed it had to be. Perhaps for her it did, and from my experience when the kids leave home there is something waiting for you to discover about yourself and the next stage in your life.

It happened to me and I believe it is part of the natural cycle of our lives, especially a women's life because of her conditioning. What was important to me (at the time and still is) is that we as women don't need to fear it, and that we have the compassion to help our partners understand it doesn't have to mean we leave them behind. It means when we are supported during this time of change we are able to love them on a much deeper level, so they need not fear. We were born, became conditioned, and finally returned to who we were born to be.

Long after I stepped into my true self and transcended my fears, my husband said to me: "So let me get this right, I met you, we married, we had kids, you changed to bring up the kids, they left, then you returned to the girl I married?"

"Yup, that's about it," I said.

Then he said: "So why would I have a problem with that?"

I answered: "Gee, I don't know but it seemed like you did at times and it almost scared me back to staying small and hiding my true self."

It took courage for me to transcend the fears I had to finally discover all of me and what and who I had come into this life to be. I couldn't have known where my journey would take me. I was afraid of the unknown, but I knew I had to do it anyway. I had to transcend my fear.

It's the balance of feminine and masculine energy within each one of us, male and female, that we are seeking in ourselves to help heal us and our world; and finally, to create peace and harmony for this is what our hearts so desire.

My dad was searching for the same thing, the balance between feminine and masculine within himself, who was he beyond ego? Rest in peace dad. All your detective work, throughout your own life, has helped me on my own journey. I got a head start from you so thank you, and I know through my writing that you have been there lighting my way to find what we were both in search of: ourselves. All those tears you had for our world were because you didn't have the tools or the words to explain to me what it was that saddened you: but I now know, you hurt for us, all of us. You knew that this journey was hard and many wouldn't want to attempt its rocky roads and that saddened you.

It's what Deepak Chopra writes in his new book, *God:* "We gave up complete authenticity in order to stay safe and sane." I know that it was time to step into all of me. This has been my journey in this life so far and to share it with you, my readers, so that you too will understand that it's why we are here, to step into our authentic selves.

EPILOGUE

Song: "Imagine" by John Lennon

It was the end of October 2012 and I felt this chapter of my life close. I felt the rising energy leave my body and in its wake I sensed a calmness, a knowing that I had finally achieved what I set out to do: I learned how to stand in my own truth and teach my children how to stand in theirs. The catalyst for this closure was seeing my daughter's ability to finally transcend the fear to speak her truth within her relationship.

She cared for her partner deeply. She always saw the truth of who he was, even when he couldn't. She had surely followed in her mother's footsteps. It took great courage for my daughter to finally let go. She, too, believed if she loved him enough he would one day wake up. If she conformed and kept the peace, he would see the truth of who he was and then she could be all of who she was. She was waiting for her partner to heal and evolve so it would be safe for her to come out and be all of herself. She finally understood that you can't wake up anyone else. It doesn't matter how much you love them, how much you conform, how much you keep yourself small or how much you keep the peace. It doesn't help. It is their choice and responsibility alone. We must learn the only way to help others is to first wake up ourselves; then this will lead the way for them to become their authentic selves too. When we live authentically, we don't have a need for attachments to others, or for them to be anything other than what they are. We lose the fear and the need to protect ourselves. This is true freedom - not only do we love ourselves unconditionally, but we're able to love others that way too. We see others at their core and know how they behave is a result of their wounds. Our job was never to fix, perhaps, if we can help them to discover their wounds and where they came from they can become the detectives in their own lives too, just as we became the detectives of our own.

I was inspired by Anthony DeMello's book, "The Way to Love". He explains that the act of seeing truth is probably the most painful experience for a person. He believes that once you begin to see, your sensitivity will make you aware of everything around you and not just the things you choose. Your wounded ego will feel its defenses weaken and will try to block the sensitivity to protect you from the truth. Only when you allow yourself to see will you then be able to understand that it has been your wounded ego that has stopped you from life and living: it has kept you stuck in a pattern. With this new awareness of being able to see all of ourselves, we can begin to understand why our ego has tried to protect us and once we understand that fact we can let go and move forward. With this new awareness of the power the ego had over us and why it is there, now comes a freedom that fills us with joy and love; thus, we are now able to relax into being our true selves.

Perhaps for my daughter her waking up was just this, the understanding and awareness of her wounded ego and the ability to stand in her truth, which she has surely done. Finally, she has listened to her inner voice.

My journey was to learn to stick up for myself and lead by example so that others, particularly my children, could do the same. It was something my parents never managed to teach me, but how could they? They were never taught themselves. This pattern in our family had to stop. I wanted my children to live happy lives based on the truths of their authentic selves. I did not want them to feel as though they had to keep themselves small or conform just to be loved. The second part I had to learn was to see how I was being in my relationship with my husband. I finally understood that by not speaking my truth it was the very thing keeping him from evolving and preventing me from becoming my authentic self. I held the strings and didn't even know it. I had gotten it all backwards.

**I didn't believe I was allowed to be me
and keep my relationship.**

Women tend to complain that men don't communicate well, but I discovered I wasn't being honest. Men say what they're thinking, yet we criticise them for it. Women don't tell the truth because we have been conditioned to think it will hurt someone's feelings or we are afraid of conflict or both. Perhaps the secret to peace and happiness for our world is the truth. Perhaps the adjustment that's required is learning how to speak our truth from a courageous, compassionate, and inquisitive way without using anger or fear for control. It takes courage to be honest and to stand in our own truth and unless we work towards healing our wounded egos, we will not be able to uncover our authentic selves. I believe we discover our wounds when we are in a relationship because our partners will surely be the trigger. Yet, how women have been communicating with men has prevented not only men from evolving but women too. In our own way we have been protecting them from themselves in believing we were keeping the peace, but really protecting ourselves, because we are afraid of conflict. I can say *we*, because I have spoken to so many women and their number one complaint about men is their inability to communicate from a detached, fearless place and this is what upsets us, puts us back in our own fears and keeps us conforming.

My husband and I became a co-dependent couple: One needing peace, conforming to get it; the other needing love, taking it from the other. These were the emotions each of us triggered within the other. I had a fear of waking up the ego in Trevor and he had a fear of being abandoned by me. Whenever we felt these wounds coming up, we would go into fear and find a way to disperse them, never being conscious enough to really understand what was happening. It wasn't until our children left that I realized I had spent most of the previous twenty years protecting myself as well as others. I still wasn't getting what I needed, which was peace and this sent me on a journey to find out why. I wasn't being honest because my wounds were controlling my choices; it's what I needed to feel safe, not what was needed. I have come to know it's essential to always speak your truth. It doesn't matter how it will be received but until you do, you will never be able to reach your authentic self or uncover the true gift of you. In telling your truths, you will learn, grow, and understand what all your wounds are. You can't grow by remaining silent and alone. It is within relationships that we learn who we really are. The people in my life who taught me the most about myself were the ones I was in conflict with, so you see if I had kept myself safe and protected my whole life, I would never have been able to step into my authentic self and I would never have been able to share my "Ah ha" moments with the world.

Growing is hard work, that's why relationships are challenging, but I want to leave you with this:

As I see it, when we understand the reason we are in a relationship (sister, brother, mother, wife, husband, father, son, daughter, friend, business) is to grow, to become our authentic selves and to realize that our experiences help us to learn about our trigger points and what we need to know about ourselves and our fears: will we evolve. Once we lose the fear of living and stop protecting ourselves from life, then we will truly be alive.

Behind vulnerability lies joy in its purest form and there is intimacy in expressing our truths so go for it. Start by telling your partner, family, and others that you have changed. You have come to the realization you don't always speak your truth for fear of conflict or? Or maybe like me, you don't even know why, but you're going on a journey to find out and you would like it if he or she would be patient and help out by not reacting to the changes in you. Explain how you now understand you are in a relationship to help unpack your bags, become detectives in your lives, not for control, but to get in touch with the authentic self and be finally free to enjoy the fullness of yourself and each other. Your individual gift will only surface once you live authentically. Don't be afraid of your truth, don't pretty it up, deliver it as it is and don't judge it for judgment is a block. Let them know that during this time your responses will be different, but that you are asking them not to react, but to try and help you understand what is going on within you. As they observe you, they will start to observe themselves. The gift is that eventually you both get to be one hundred percent you and then you can enjoy each other too!

Remember the movie Slum dog Millionaire. What if this thing we call "life" is just a game? What if we are creating our own play and we get to choose all the players in our play? What if all the players are just helping us to evolve into consciousness. As in the movie *Slum dog Millionaire,* in which the unique life experiences of the main character helped him win one million on a game show? Was he conscious he was playing the game of life? What if you could be conscious in your own game of life? Imagine what kind of life that could bring to you?

My mind is quiet these days. When I speak my truth, I don't wonder if it will be met with conflict because it doesn't matter how it's met any longer. The only thing that drives me is always saying exactly what I'm thinking, no matter what, but in a kind way with a calm voice and fearless energy. This is how I will continue to learn and to grow. This is how being my authentic self will lead the way for others to become theirs.

As Eliza Mada Dalian mentions in her book, *In Search of the Miraculous: Healing into Consciousness*, "Each one of us is responsible for searching and finding the original face for ourselves. To uncover it, we must embrace the present moment and the unknown it contains. The miraculous is the unknown, which is always revealed moment to moment in the stillness of the present."

When we come to understand we are all a part of a whole and instead of trying to protect ourselves from what we are afraid of, when we learn to help each other overcome our fears, then we will see the beauty of the moment and of each other.

It's time to take off the mask and uncover our truths so we may be free to truly live.

As my father used to say: "I am, the I, that I am." Broken down to our smallest common denominator, we are a seed made from love.

Namaste Chental

After my husband finished reading my book he sent me an email and said the following:

"Wow well done. You really do know how to put it. I love you so much it hurts and then mostly I am in awe of your wisdom even though sometimes its hurts when you are so honest, I love you even more for it.

It is getting time to go again as I love the oneness that we are while on the road. I also get to have you all to myself, I know that is wrong but I am speaking my truth. I feel we are so much together and I love you for everything you are in me.

Trev "

Resources

Thankyou and credit goes out to all the great authors before me who have helped me in my own journey.

Book Title: Spontaneous Evolution
Author: Bruce H. Lipton, Ph.D and Steve Bhaerman
ISBN:978-1-4019-2631-1
Copyright date:2009
Publisher:Hay House Inc., Carlsbad, CA

Book Title:The Biology of Belief
Author:Bruce H. Lipton, Ph.D
ISBN:978-1-4019-2311-2
Copyright Date:2008
Publisher:Hay House Inc.,Carlsbad, CA

Book Title:A New Earth
Author:Eckhart Tolle
ISBN:0-525-94802-3
Copyright date:2005
Publisher:Namaste Publishing, Vancouver, B.C. Canada

Book Title:Dying To Be Me
Author:Anita Moorjani
ISBN:978-1-4019-3751-5
Copyright date:2012
Publisher:Hay House Inc., Carlsbad, CA

Book Title:Article in a Magazine
Quoted from Lynn Woodward of
Namaste Publishing in an article.
Namaste Publishing, Vancouver, B.C.

Book Title:The Top Five Regrets of the Dying
Author:Bronnie Ware
ISBN:978-1-45250-234-2
Copyright date:2011
Publisher:Hay House Inc., Carlsbad, CA

Book:Verse in her training manual "The Language of the Body"
Author:Helen Belot Sekhem
Copyright date:1999
Published:Self Published Queensland Australia

Book Title:The Book of Secrets Unlocking the Hidden
Dimensions of Your Life
Author:Deepak Chopra
ISBN:1-4000-9834-3
Copyright date:2004
Publisher:Three Rivers an imprint of the Crown Publishing
Group, division of Random House, Inc., New York.

Book Title:Adrenal Fatigue The 21st Century Stress Syndrome
Author:James L Wilson, N.D.,D.C.,Ph.D.
ISBN:1-890572-15-2
Copyright Date: 2001
Publisher:Smart Publications
URL: http://www.smart-publications.com/books/
adrenal-fatigue-the-21st-century-stress-syndrome

Book:In Search of the Miraculous Healing Into Consciousness
Author:Eliza Mada Dalian
ISBN:978-0-9738773-2-8
Copyright Date:2008
Publisher:Expanding Universe Publishing, PO Box 19168,
Vancouver, B.C. V6K 4R8
URL: http://madadalian.com/

Book:Awakening into Oneness:The Power of Blessing in the Evolution of Consciousness
Author:Arjuna Ardagh
ISBN:978-1-59179-573-5
Copyright Date:
Publisher:Sounds True Publishing, Boulder Co.

Book:Online response on his page to me. I & I Discoveries
Author:Master Dhyan Vimal
http://www.dhyanvimal-iandi.com/

Book Title:Smile at Fear Awakening the True Heart of Bravery
Author:Chogyam Trungpa
ISBN:978-1-59030-696-3
Copyright Date:2009
Publisher:Shambhala Publishers, http://www.shambhala.com

Book Title:The Way to Love – The Last Meditations of Anthony De Mello
Author:Anthony De Mello
ISBN: 0-385-24939-X
Copyright Date:1995
Publisher:Published by Doubleday a div of Random House Publishing

Book Title:Warrior of the Light A Manual
Author:Paulo Coelho
ISBN:0-06-052797-8
Copyright Date:2003
Publisher:Harper Collins Publishers Inc., 10 East 53rd Street, New York NY 10022

Book Title:As You Think – The self-empowerment classic As
A Man Thinketh revised and updated by Marc Allen
Author: James Allen
ISBN: 978-1-57731-074-7
Copyright:1998
Publisher:Publishers Group - West New World Library, CA.

Author Biography

Born in High Wycombe, England, into a strong Catholic family, Chental is the second youngest of nine girls. She met her husband at the age of fifteen and was married at nineteen. They immigrated to Toronto, Canada in 1981, moved to B.C. a year later to start a family and a family business with her sister and brother-in-law. They have two children.

After twenty eight years of being part of the business she decided that there must be 'More'. Her husband was game for a change too, so they took a year off, sold their house and travelled around the world on his motorcycle, seeing thirty countries in fourteen months; this was indeed a life changing experience for them both. Sitting on the back of that bike gave her time to reflect on her life and experiences.

Today she lives on Salt Spring Island with her husband and this is her first book, she decided she couldn't keep what she had learnt on her own journey through life to herself, it was her responsibility to share it.

More About Chental Wilson

Chental and her work:
www.chentalwilson.com

Contact Chental for speaking engagements:
chentalwilson@yahoo.ca

To purchase her books go to her Facebook page or Amazon.

For educational videos, podcasts, interviews etc...
www.chentalwilson.com for the links
www.inspiredauthorscircle.com/chental-wilson

Chental is a member of Friends to Mankind:
www.friendstomankind.org

And a member at: Are you a messenger of change:
www.areyouamessenger.com

My travelling blog:
www.trevsblogg.blogspot.ca

Contact her publisher:
Julie Salisbury
Founder and Facilitator InspireABook
Founder Influence Publishing
contact@influencepublishing.com
www.influencepublishing.com
Check out our next book launch at:
www.inspiredauthorscircle.com
skype: inspireabook

Chental supports the following charities at this time and a percentage of profits will go to these charities, see the links on her website.

Because I am a girl:
www.becauseiamagirl.ca

The Equality Effect:
www.theequalityeffect.org

Thank you for all your support. In the purchasing of this book, you have supported these girls and the education that is so desperately needed in our world.

"When awareness grows, and you become clearly alert, acceptance is a natural consequence"

If you want to get on the path to be a published author by **Influence Publishing** please go to
www.InspireABook.com

Inspiring books that influence change

More information on our other titles and how to submit your own proposal can be found at
www.InfluencePublishing.com

CPSIA information can be obtained at www.ICGtesting.com
Printed in the USA
LVOW05s2344260914

406097LV00005B/18/P